Seeking the Mystery

Seeking the Mystery

An Introduction to Pagan Theologies

Christine Hoff Kraemer

Patheos Press | Englewood, CO

for my students
and for those they will teach

1st edition
Published by Patheos Press
Englewood, Colorado

12 13 14 15 16 17 18 19 20 21—10 9 8 7 6 5 4 3 2 1

Cover design by Shatter

Library of Congress Cataloging-in-Publication Data

Kraemer, Christine Hoff.
    Seeking the Mystery: An Introduction to Pagan Theologies. Includes bibliographical references.
    ISBN: 978-1-939221-18-6 (alk. paper)

PRINTED IN THE UNITED STATES OF AMERICA

For information, contact Patheos Press, 383 Inverness Parkway, Suite 260, Englewood CO 80112, or contact us online at
www.patheos.com/Books/Patheos-Press.

Contents

Introduction

Pagan Theologies

When I taught my first course in contemporary Pagan theology, I opened the class by asking my students why they had enrolled. One of my brightest and most articulate students—a professional woman who already had her first Master's degree—described her visit to A Parliament of the World's Religions, an enormous interfaith dialogue conference that she had attended as one of about fifty contemporary Pagans. "When people asked me what Pagans believe, I was tongue-tied," she said. "I need to know how to answer that question."

My student's problem wasn't that she didn't understand her own religion. The problem was that she was being asked a question that is rarely discussed in contemporary Paganism. Especially for Protestant readers, the question "What do you *believe?*" probably seems like the first and most important thing to ask about any religion. Most interfaith dialogue in the United States begins with a discussion of beliefs, and even the term "interfaith" demonstrates the degree to which, for English speakers, *religion* is defined in terms of *faith* (belief). For Pagans, however, practice is at the center of their religious lives; shared practice, not shared belief, is what ties groups together.

Nor is Paganism the only minority religion in the West to emphasize practice over belief. Jewish communities can be equally diverse, with some practitioners primarily attending synagogue because of a belief in God, and others to honor their ancestors and their culture. When the focus is on ritual and community rather than on belief, the members of a congregation may go years or even a lifetime without ever thinking to ask about others' motivations for attendance. Similarly, attendees of Hindu devotional rites may hold a wide variety of beliefs about what the proceedings mean. Those with a philosophical bent may understand the gods as principles, archetypes, or metaphors for the forces of nature; others may be passionate devotees of the gods and believe in their personal intervention in their families' lives; still others may participate as a way of maintaining contact with their ethnic heritage and culture. In all these cases, group participation in ritual helps to maintain a community of mutual support. Religion becomes less about what people believe about the divine or the nature of the world, and more about how they behave.

The Pagan group with whom I do seasonal celebrations is typical. In many ways, we have a common worldview: many of us work in education, and we have similar political commitments and share a love of the outdoors. Yet we hardly discuss our metaphysical beliefs, and on the rare occasions that we do, there is little common ground. To one, the God/dess is a higher power within and outside ourselves, but s/he is unknowable; the named gods are metaphors we use to address something too big for us to comprehend. To another, the gods are objectively existing beings with whom we can have a relationship, but who are evolving and changing just as human beings are. A third explains that she believes in the literal existence of the gods in ritual, but tends toward agnosticism in daily life; a fourth, when pressed, prefers to identify as a Buddhist, but participates in Pagan ritual because "it's what my community does."

When asked what Pagans believe, my student found herself tongue-tied partially because Pagans focus on their practices, not their beliefs. But the question is also difficult because Paganism is so diverse. As in the group I celebrate with, practitioners may hold radically different beliefs about the nature of the divine, the possibility of an afterlife, the meaning of shared ritual actions, and other seemingly key religious issues, all while relating to a single body of liturgy and ritual. Contemporary Paganism includes hundreds of groups and traditions, each with their own ritual practices. Wicca is the largest contemporary Pagan tradition and in itself contains dozens of lineages. Other traditions include Ásatrú or Heathenry (Northern European Paganism), Druidry, feminist Goddess spirituality, non-Wiccan forms of religious witchcraft, and reconstructionism (the attempt to recreate ancient religions such as those of Greece and Egypt; some Heathens also view their religion as reconstructionist). Paganism can also be part of an ethnic or national identity, as in Eastern Europe, where Baltic Pagans are reviving the religious elements of folk traditions; some practitioners of Afro-Caribbean religions also identify as Pagan, though most do not. Further, not all Pagans belong to traditions. Pagans can practice as *solitaries* (by themselves) or *eclectics* (drawing from many traditions). Although some pieces of liturgy, such as Doreen Valiente's well-known "Charge of the Goddess," are used in many different contemporary Pagan traditions, it is possible—even easy!—to find two Pagan practitioners who do not share a word of liturgy, nor a single practice.

Pagans often actively resist defining "Pagan" or "Paganism." Most Pagans were raised as Christians or Jews (although this is changing as Pagan parents raise their children as Pagans). Many left the religions of their birth due to theological and ethical disagreements or, in some cases, traumatic experiences. As a result, Pagans can be suspicious of organized religion and of anything that smacks of dogma or prescriptive doctrine. Standardized definitions of Paganism strike some Pagans as a threat to the authenticity and spontaneity of their religious practice.

One might ask at this point, "What use is the label 'Pagan' if those calling themselves Pagan have so little in common?" The answer is that despite a great diversity in beliefs and practices, there are recurring attitudes and behaviors that meaningfully unite contemporary Pagan traditions into a religious movement (rather than a single religion). Although the only trait that *all* Pagans share may be the use of the word "Pagan," *most* Pagans hold *most* of the following attitudes.

- **Pantheism, panentheism, or animism**. Pagans experience divinity in the physical world. Pantheists see the world itself as a deity ("All is God/dess"). Panentheists believe that deity is present throughout the material world, but see deity as more than just the world itself ("God/dess is in all things, and all things are in God/dess"). Animists see a spirit or soul in all things (or sometimes, all natural things), and may or may not acknowledge a unifying deity.

- **Polytheism**. Pagans honor multiple gods and goddesses in their religious practice. Some Pagans are *soft polytheists* and see the many gods as aspects of one God/dess, as aspects of a Goddess and a God, as Jungian archetypes, or as metaphors for natural forces. Others are *hard polytheists* and understand the gods as individual beings, separate and unique in the same way that human beings are.
- **Reverence toward nature and the body**. "Pagan" comes from the Latin *paganus,* which probably meant "a person from a rural area." For many, the word "Pagan" reflects a nature-oriented spirituality. Accordingly, Pagans often celebrate natural cycles and may be passionate environmentalists. The body and sexuality are treated as a sacred part of nature. (See also *ecotheology*.)
- **Reference to pre-Christian myths and traditions and/or indigenous traditions**. Pagans look to pre-Christian religions, or to religions that have resisted conversion to Christianity, for ways to connect to the land, to themselves, or to the gods/the divine.
- **Ritual practice**. Pagan identity comes from the practice of ritual. Rituals may celebrate the seasons, the cycles of the moon, or the accomplishments of one's ancestors; honor a deity or deities; or mark life transitions such as births, deaths, and weddings. Pagan rituals often employ drumming; dance; ceremonial fires; incense; physical representations of earth, air, fire, and water; or other sensory elements.
- **Trust in personal experience as a source of divine knowledge** (sometimes called *gnosis*). With some exceptions, Pagans give personal experiences more

authority than texts or received tradition. They emphasize intuition and knowledge felt in the body.

- **Acknowledgement of the principles of magick**. Many Pagans believe that ritual acts performed with intention can alter consciousness, and therefore, reality. Such rituals function similarly to prayer in other religions. Pagans who practice magick often refer to themselves as *witches* or *magicians*.

- **Virtue ethics**. Pagan ethical principles often focus on relationships, and ethics are tailored to individual situations. Virtues and values are considered more important than inflexible rules. Most Pagans value cultivating the self, one's community, and the earth while avoiding harm to others. Celebration, community service, creativity, harmony, and love are often emphasized. Pagans who look to ancient warrior traditions, such as Germanic and Celtic cultures, may instead stress honor, truth, courage, and fidelity.

- **Pluralism**. Pagans usually consider the traditions of other religions to be as potentially legitimate as their own. No one spiritual path can be right for everyone because people have different spiritual needs.[1]

Even as I lay out what appears to be a definition, however, I want to be clear that these are not *defining* characteristics of contemporary Paganism. Rather, they are *emergent* patterns of behavior and belief that I have observed in my fifteen years in the contemporary Pagan community— commonalities that cut across lines of group and tradition. I do not intend this list to be employed as a litmus test for whether a group or individual is Pagan. Many Pagan groups may share only five or six of these qualities, and which five or six will vary from group to group. However, I point out these qualities so that Pagans might gain clarity about what makes Pagan community attractive—why Pagans feel more at home among other self-identified Pagans than we do in other religious communities.

I also hope to give non-Pagans a starting point from which to approach a religious movement that might otherwise look dizzyingly varied. Despite some genuinely deep theological differences within the Pagan community, these recurring qualities help to distinguish Pagan traditions as a group from other new religious movements, such as the New Age. Further, perhaps naming these commonalities will give non-Pagans ideas for fruitful interfaith dialogue. Paganism has already served as a provocative dialogue partner for progressive Christians and Jews around issues of environmentalism and sexuality; what might Pagans and Buddhists, Pagans and Mormons, or Pagans and Muslims have to say to each other?

This introduction to contemporary Pagan theology—or more properly, *theologies*—is not meant to be definitive, nor can it ever be. The strength of contemporary Pagan theology is that it constantly evolves. Theology—the study of deity—is something we *do,* a practice by which we grow in understanding of our relationships with the divine, with other human beings, and with the world. It is not a matter of mere theory, but a process that calls us to make connections between reason and experience, between history and contemporary life, between our own practices and those of others. In search of authentic spiritual experience, contemporary Pagans have focused on ritual, with effective results. Yet in its suspicion of organized religion and dogma, Paganism has not always recognized the reciprocal relationship of practice and belief: practices arise out of attitudes, and beliefs arise from the experience of practice. Discussions of contemporary Pagan belief need not end in routinization and the creation of doctrine. Rather, Pagan theology can include expressions of our most sacred encounters, the lingering impressions of our holiest experiences. Remaining open to new encounters with the divine, Pagans seek to retain access to mystery: experiential knowledge of the sacred that changes from individual to individual, from time to time, and from culture to culture. The wisdom of Pagan theology is in its flexibility, its willingness to honor and remember the past while seeking to engage the present moment.

Associating theological terms with Christianity, Pagans have sometimes resisted the entire idea of Pagan theology. Yet the standard theological terms that we use in Western religion all have a pre-Christian origin in ancient Greece. Contemporary Paganism is only now beginning to develop a body of theological literature, a process that requires synthesizing the inheritance of ancient religions with modern ethical and spiritual understandings. Sadly, there is not space to explore ancient theologies here. Instead, this book will create a small intellectual bridge between the ancient world and the present by helping readers learn basic theological terms in a contemporary Pagan context.

Becoming a Theologian

I have an academic background in religious studies and theology. As long as I only did theology by reading books and writing papers, though, I never considered myself to be a theologian. After an intense five years in graduate school, I committed to seeking initiation in the non-Wiccan tradition of religious witchcraft that I had been studying for several years. Around the same time, I enrolled in massage therapy school and learned (or perhaps remembered) how to truly be present in my body.

In my Craft tradition, the body holds a connection to the primal past that all humans share. Culture and technology have changed radically since the Stone Age, but the realities of the human body remain the same. In ritual, I learned to engage the natural resources of my body, first to understand what it is to be human, and through the human, to also know divinity. In the midst of the many life changes that followed, I found my theological voice.

Slowly, I began to return to my intellectual work: I was hired as an instructor at Cherry Hill Seminary, which provides online community and graduate-level training in Pagan ministry and scholarship. While serving as chair of the Theology and Religious History department, I also developed the core theology class that all Master's students at the seminary take. The class was more than an intellectual exercise, though. It was an expression of the questions I had grappled with in my spiritual life, and an invitation for my students to struggle similarly, and perhaps even come to different answers.

Today, I am a teacher, a massage therapist (now very part-time), and an initiated witch. I am also a Pagan theologian—not because I write books about theology, but because my experiments in belief and practice have given me a life infused with sacred presence. I became a theologian the first time I tried to explain the lived experience of my religion to someone else. Although I will share a little of my personal theology in this book, my larger goal is to enable others' voices: to provide a vocabulary for belief, and a framework to investigate the place where belief and practice meet.

Victor Anderson, an American teacher of the Craft, was fond of saying, "Perceive first, then believe." In our movement from religious experience to religious belief, we are all theologians. If you are a Pagan, I hope this book will help you elaborate on your personal theology and that of your community. And if you are a practitioner of another religion or of no religion at all, I hope that this exploration of an alternative religious path will both challenge and deepen your own spirituality.

How to Use This Book

Since theology is an activity, readers are invited to try on the role of theologian. Each chapter includes suggestions for exercises and experiments to help readers explore Pagan theological concepts (Activities). Although the activities were designed with the individual in mind, they are equally well-suited for discussion or ritual groups to try together. To assist readers in digesting the material, every chapter also includes a synopsis of its contents (Summary), as well as a brief bibliography of recommended books and essays in each topic area (Further Reading). The book also includes a Glossary defining both theological terms and important concepts in Paganism. Readers who are making heavy use of the Glossary may wish to open it in a separate window or print it out for quick reference.

Those who are entirely new to Paganism may find it challenging to distinguish between the many paths and theological positions I mention here. Readers who want to familiarize themselves with the many traditions of Paganism should begin with the most recent edition of Margot Adler's *Drawing Down the Moon,* a journalistic exploration that is smart, engaging, and written by an insider.

A Note on Language

The English language is notoriously lacking when it comes to gender-neutral pronouns. Many readers find that using "he or she" or "they" as singular nouns quickly becomes awkward. Attempts are being made to add gender-neutral pronouns such as "zhe" to English, and I have used those neologisms myself when discussing gender theory. However, these new terms have not caught on widely outside of gender studies. I feel that in this context, their use is likely to distract readers who are unfamiliar with them. Accordingly, I have alternated the use of "he" and "she" when referring to a hypothetical individual who could be of any gender.

I have also used the term "magick" as coined by early twentieth-century magician Aleister Crowley (note the pronunciation of his name is like the bird, "crow"). Crowley preferred the alternative spelling in order to differentiate ceremonial magick from stage magic. Today, the term "magick" is used widely (but not universally) by Pagans. I employ it here to emphasize that magick in Paganism is a set of spiritual practices. It should not be confused with the fanciful "magic" portrayed in fantasy novels and films.

Overview

We begin with an exploration of the nature of divinity in contemporary Paganism. *Chapter One: Deity, Deities, and the Divine* is dense with theological terminology—readers should not despair if they cannot learn every term on the first read-through!

Chapter Two: Myth, Tradition, and Innovation discusses myth as the context for divine-human relationships. In Paganism, myths are sacred stories that structure practice and belief. The chapter discusses narratives that are commonly used among Pagans, as well as the question of what makes a Pagan tradition authentic.

Chapter Three: Knowledge and Devotion presents some of the techniques with which Pagans pursue human-divine relationships. Pagans use ritual practices to seek *gnosis* (knowledge gained from extraordinary sources), as well as to demonstrate commitment and devotion to the God/dess or the gods.

Chapter Four: Life, Death, and the Human Body focuses on the nature of being human. The chapter introduces the role of sex and gender in contemporary Pagan traditions, the makeup of the human soul (or souls!), and the practice of ancestor veneration.

Chapter Five: Ethics and Justice tackles the issue of right relationship between and among human beings. The chapter looks at the use of virtue-based ethical systems in contemporary Paganism and considers whether "evil" is a valid concept in Pagan theology.

Finally, the *Conclusion* looks ahead to the rapid evolution of Paganism in the twenty-first century.

Further Reading

Adler, Margot. *Drawing Down the Moon: Witches, Druids, Goddess-Worshippers, and Other Pagans in America*. Revised and Updated. New York: Penguin, 2006.

Harvey, Graham. *Contemporary Paganism: Religions of the Earth from Druids and Witches to Heathens and Ecofeminists.* New York: NYU Press, 2011.

Strmiska, Michael, ed. *Modern Paganism in World Cultures: Comparative Perspectives.* Santa Barbara, CA: ABC-CLIO, 2005.

Chapter One

Deity, Deities, and the Divine

The key to contemporary Pagan understanding of deities and divinity is multiplicity.

As we know already, contemporary Pagans are diverse in belief and practice; Paganism has *theologies* rather than one theology. Since Pagan experiences of the divine are inherently personal and individual, practitioners are not required to maintain loyalty to one particular theology if their experiences of the divine shift. Some Pagans may change aspects of their theology over the course of a lifetime, or they may change from day to day depending on context (like the friend I mentioned in the introduction, who is a theist when in circle but an agnostic otherwise). For Pagans, theology is not fixed, but rather an ongoing intellectual engagement with spiritual processes.

The most common definition of "theology" is "the study of God/the gods." In the West, we tend to associate theological study with attending seminary and poring over difficult philosophical texts. Yet examining what our predecessors thought and believed about their gods is only one way to study the divine. Pagans are often voracious readers and do look for information about the gods or the God/dess in books. But theology can also be undertaken with an experimental method and an exploratory attitude, much like a naturalist encountering the wild.

The starting place for any individual Pagan's theology is the personal spiritual experience. As Pagans, we ask ourselves: What makes me feel uplifted, connected, deeply compassionate, or ecstatically joyful? What helps me to cope with the anxieties or pressures of everyday life and present my best self to the world? When has my breath caught from an upwelling of beauty, or when have I been shaken to my core by awe? These questions help to pinpoint the foundational spiritual encounters that often arise spontaneously, yet can be easily forgotten without a practice that puts them into context. Seeking out such spiritual experiences and integrating them into a fulfilling life is a vital way that Pagans do theology.

The importance of multiplicity in Pagan concepts of the divine may seem unusual in Western religious culture, where *monotheism* (belief in only one deity) is considered the norm. Yet many of the world's other religious traditions also have multiple and changing notions about the nature of deity. Although contemporary Pagans have beliefs and practices that can be challenging for monotheists to relate to, there are also points of overlap from which Pagans and those of other faiths can begin satisfying theological conversations. Accordingly, I will begin with those theological points of view that are likely to be most familiar to non-Pagan readers: those that connect to wider conversations in American theology.

The reader will notice that I switch freely between "the divine," "God/dess," "the gods," and other terms in this section. I do this partly to reflect the views of the writers and theologians I will be discussing, and partly because none of these terms successfully encompasses the others. Within Paganism are practitioners who reject even the vaguely indicated oneness of saying "the divine," and others who are uncomfortable with the separateness and distinction implied by "the gods." As we will see, these two incompatible perspectives are linked by a theological middle ground where the majority of contemporary Pagans find themselves on a day-to-day basis.

Feminist Theology

Contemporary Paganism has been profoundly influenced by writers who were part of the spiritual feminist movement (sometimes also called the Goddess spirituality movement). Particularly in the 1970s and 1980s, much of the sophisticated writing about feminine images of divinity came from theologians who were part of a larger political movement to secure equal rights for women. This spiritual feminist movement was the precursor of the queer spirituality movement that is flourishing today. Although the feminist and queer spirituality movements have some philosophical differences around gender and sexuality, both are committed to egalitarianism, collective social justice, and personal liberation.

Some of these writers considered themselves to be Pagans or witches; others remained progressive Christians or Jews, while yet others saw themselves as "post-Christian." Post-Christian Goddess worshippers have been deeply influenced by Christianity, and they are still engaged with Christian ideas and symbolism. They may feel deeply wounded by Christian theology—especially Christian theologies that denigrate women, sexuality, and the human body—or they may simply see their practice as too different from that of mainstream Christian groups to be accurately called "Christian." Accordingly, many writers in the Goddess movement write for an audience that includes Pagans, but is not limited to them. In order to emphasize that their writings are exploring feminine divinity and female ways of knowing the Goddess, many feminist writers adopted the term "thealogy" for their work.

For a variety of reasons, I choose not to use the term "thealogy" here. I agree with feminist thealogians that the term "thealogy" forces readers to constantly consider the possibility of a feminine deity, one whose nature may be radically different from the standard Western idea of God. Thealogy also employs methods and models that are different from mainstream Western theology. But there are many forms of progressive "theology" that are quite similar to "thealogy" (feminist, queer, and process theologies, for instance). To switch back and forth between "thealogy" and "theology" would suggest that thealogy is a completely separate system of thought, rather than one among many related theological viewpoints. I hope that readers will come away from this book with the original Greek sense of "theology" as a word that need not refer to a single deity, nor solely to a masculine one.

Process Theology

Carol Christ has been one of the strongest voices for post-Christian Goddess worship. Her theology has changed somewhat since 1978, when she gave her influential lecture "Why Women Need the Goddess" at the University of Santa Cruz.[1] Although her earlier works focus passionately on women and their spirituality, in her most recent book, *She Who Changes,* social justice around gender is only one of her concerns. Christ was educated in theology at Yale University, where she studied *process thought,* an important twentieth-century philosophical and theological movement. In process thought, the divine is believed to be constantly in a process of becoming and changing. Deity is *immanent* in the world, fully present and involved in all of being—expressed in people and animals, plants and rocks, the stars in the heavens and the dust beneath our feet. This idea is in contrast to traditional Western ideas of the divine being eternal, unchanging, and *transcendent,* fundamentally beyond the physical world. For process theologians, neither reality nor God/dess is finished or complete. In fact, the changeability of our selves, our consciousness, our society, and our earth are an active part of an ongoing divine creation.

Some process theologians are *pantheists,* meaning that they see God/dess as the world itself and the world itself as God/dess. Some contemporary ecotheologians hold a similar view, believing that the complex ecosystem that sustains us—and that human beings are now altering so dramatically—is itself the divine process of creation. Pantheists may or may not believe that the Earth has an emergent consciousness or will that calls us to compassionate, holistic living. It is more common, however, for process theologians to consider themselves *panentheists.* Panentheists believe that God/dess is within all things of the world, but that God/dess is also *more* than the world and contains it. Panentheists vary in how they understand this transcendent aspect of God/dess, but the idea that the divine is "more than the sum of its parts" expresses believers' experience of a divinity fundamentally greater than themselves.

For those who seek ethical guidance from the divine, the idea that part of God/dess is outside the world as well as part of it fits well with the notion that there is a divine plan or intention for creation. Rather than seeing God/dess as exploring and changing as blindly as human beings often feel they do, God/dess is seen as a full participant in the world, yet possessing the objectivity to influence and shape it.

Seeing the world as constantly in process is common in Pagan theology. This view is captured in Starhawk's well-known chant, "She changes everything she touches, and everything she touches changes." But these ideas also appear in other religious traditions, where the concepts of process thought and evolutionary theory often go together. French Jesuit and paleontologist Pierre Teilhard de Chardin, for example, embraced the work of Darwin and used it as the primary lens through which he saw divine creation. In addition to his scientific studies, he produced gorgeous poetry celebrating the awe and majesty of the natural world, often in process terms. "'Nature,'" he writes, "is the equivalent of 'becoming,' self-creation: this is the view to which experience irresistibly leads us."[2] Other progressive Christian theologians have carried on Teilhard de Chardin's work, including Matthew Fox, who founded the contemporary creation spirituality movement. (Because of the similarity in names, this movement is sometimes confused with Christian creationism, to which it is almost diametrically opposed. "Creation spirituality" is an earth-focused spirituality that sees God/dess as fully immanent in an ongoing creation. "Creationism" interprets the book of Genesis literally, rejecting evolutionary theory and asserting that the world was created by God about six thousand years ago.) Fox puts creation—the physical world—at the center of his theology, and evolution is his chosen creation story. Encouraging his readers to seek out the divine through artistic creation and celebration, he actively mines the Christian tradition for writers and mystics who similarly experienced God as immanent. Fox continues to be friendly toward the Pagan movement, and Starhawk has been an instructor at his Institute for Creation Spirituality (now Wisdom University).

Soft Polytheism

Goddess theology like Christ's—perhaps because it is directed to an inherently interfaith audience—tends to slip back and forth between a modified monotheism and a position known as *soft polytheism.* Soft polytheism sees the many gods as aspects of one God/dess, or sometimes as aspects of a Goddess and a God (also called *duotheism,* or belief in a pair of deities). In its most unifying flavors, soft polytheism can look a great deal like the monotheism found in certain strands of Christianity. The Christian Trinity—Father, Son, and Holy Spirit—represents a significant division of the divine, and much ink has been spilled to explain the relationship of these three divine aspects to each other. To some thinkers within Abrahamic religions, even the Christian Trinity is problematically non-monotheistic. Catholic Christian practice especially engages multiplicity: within Catholicism, Mary the Mother of God and the saints are venerated in ways that resemble the polytheistic devotions of Hindus and Pagans. Catholics understand the saints as intercessors between human beings and God, who is too vast to be grasped by the human mind. But to polytheistic outsiders, the saints appear similar to the limited but highly approachable gods of ancient and modern polytheistic traditions. The fact that many pre-Christian deities were syncretized with Christian saints during Roman Catholic conversions adds to the polytheistic parallels.

Protestant Christianity also has theologies that attempt to draw out the many from the one. Theologian Sallie McFague, for example, advocates for *metaphorical theology*, an approach that avoids limiting believers' idea of God/dess through the use of multiple metaphors. She points out that the Christian tradition contains many images of God/dess in both feminine and masculine aspects: as mother and father, as child, and as beloved friend, one who "became flesh and pitched a tent among us."[3] In

McFague's view, a single-minded focus on images of God as lord and king has been destructive to the Christian tradition. Rather than throwing these metaphors away, she suggests an expansion where many images of the divine are honored. Despite this acceptance of diversity in images of God/dess, however, McFague's theology remains explicitly monotheistic.[4]

As we have seen, monotheism can contain a great deal of multiplicity, and soft polytheism can also accommodate a great deal of unity. Although Carol Christ sometimes speaks of named goddesses such as Diana or Kali, she tends to see the myths of polytheistic cultures as sources of "Goddess symbolism," not as tales of individual divine personalities. In *She Who Changes,* she preferentially uses the term "Goddess/God" to indicate a gender-inclusive deity that arises from divine process and can be called by many names. Christ's theology is *theistic*; she affirms that Goddess/God is an entity or consciousness with whom we can have a relationship (in other words, her Goddess/God is a personal deity). Her position, however, is at times quite similar to that of *nontheists* within contemporary Paganism.

Nontheism

I prefer the term "nontheist" to "atheist," although by dictionary definition they are essentially interchangeable. In the United States, "atheism" has become strongly associated not just with the denial of deity, but with the position that religion and spirituality are pathological and fundamentally based on delusion. "Nontheism," on the other hand, retains the more neutral meaning of "belief in a lack or absence of deity." In some cases, the word is also applied to those who acknowledge the existence of deity or deities, but who feel that those beings have no relevance to humanity.

Nontheists within Paganism may embrace the mythology and symbolism of the Goddess or the gods as tools for human empowerment. Alternately, they may interact with spirits whom they do not consider to be deities, as we will see in the section on animism. For nontheists, ritual is a deeply affecting practice that builds community, produces extraordinary states of consciousness, and can lead to individual and collective transformation.

Some nontheists understand mythology in terms of Jungian archetypes. According to twentieth-century psychologist C.G. Jung, an *archetype* is a pattern or symbol that is universal to human experience.[5] Archetypes appear in the myths and stories of all the world's cultures, which is why those who study such myths are able to find similar images and patterns in cultures that have no direct communication with each other. Jung employed the concept of archetypes to analyze the dreams of emotionally disturbed patients. This kind of therapy continues today, and it has also grown past the mere treatment of illness into a technique for spiritual exploration and development. Jung himself was a devout theist, believing that archetypes gave human beings access to a transcendent deity. In contemporary Paganism, however, archetypes are often understood as giving access to human nature, but not to anything beyond it. This purely psychological approach to archetypes is the most common form of nontheism in Paganism.

Monism

Archetypes are also used by those who believe in an underlying divine reality, but do not believe in the existence of a personal deity or deities. For these practitioners, archetypes serve as human user interfaces on a universe that is utterly inhuman. The gods or God/dess may be seen as culturally constructed filters used to access a transcendent divine reality. Some of these Pagans consider themselves to be monists. Pagan monism can be considered a type of nontheism, but it differs from the "spirituality as psychology" approach discussed above. Monism is the belief that a single divine substance underlies reality, and that despite the appearance of multiplicity and fragmentation, all things are ultimately one. Unlike those for whom archetypes are purely tools for personal empowerment or political liberation, Pagan monists take the metaphysical aspects of reality very seriously. In Pagans, monism is often based on a perception of underlying oneness and interdependence as experienced in ritual or meditation. In contrast to monism as it sometimes appears in Eastern religions, however, Pagan monism tends to remain interested in embodiment and multiplicity. Some forms of Hinduism and Buddhism condemn the appearance of separateness as a dangerous and destructive illusion. These traditions see our separateness from each other, from the world, and from being itself as sources of pain and suffering. For monist Pagans, however, there is a purpose, and more importantly a *beauty*, to our manyness that deserves our attention. Rather than seeking to leave the wheel of birth, death, and reincarnation, Pagan monists revel in it.

Monist Pagans often do not believe that ultimate reality is something with which one can have a personal, reciprocal relationship. Although the spiritual dimension of life is absolutely real—perhaps the most real thing there is—any face or personality we put on the oneness is nothing more than human perception. Other Pagans hold beliefs very similar to Pagan monists, but instead affirm that reality is made up of *two* complementary spiritual substances. Often, the goddesses and gods of the world are all considered aspects or manifestations of these two primal forces, which they call the Goddess and the God. Pagans who believe that the Goddess and the God are metaphorical—archetypes or human constructions on inexplicable divine realities—might be said to embrace *dualism* rather than monism (although this is not the only possible meaning of dualism in Paganism). Pagans who believe that one can have personal relationships with the Goddess and the God, however, would be more properly called *duotheists,* which is a form of soft polytheism.

Learning to Apply Theological Terms

Before we continue on to explore hard polytheism and animism in contemporary Paganism, let's step back for a moment to review and apply the terms we've already learned. I want to emphasize again that the purpose of defining theological terms in contemporary Paganism is to enable Pagans to have complex conversations about their beliefs and attitudes. It is not to separate Pagans into groups centered around particular beliefs, nor to set Pagans with different beliefs in opposition to each other. In a healthy spiritual life, theological positions are rarely static. Although I have spoken in general terms of Pagan theists, nontheists, and monists, I would not presume to impose these labels on individuals who did not claim them. Ultimately, these terms describe *beliefs,* not people.

I have attempted to tease apart various theological positions for the sake of clearer discussion. In practice, however, they are usually blurred: real-life spiritual experiences do not relegate themselves to cleanly defined categories. The theological writings of Pagans and Goddess worshippers often reflect hybrids of these positions, as we can see by looking at important books that shaped the Pagan movement.

Merlin Stone's groundbreaking book *When God Was a Woman* explores goddess worship in ancient cultures. It was published in the mid-1970s and had an enormous impact on the spiritual feminist and Pagan communities. Stone examines the art and mythology of ancient Near and Middle Eastern goddesses for insights about Goddess-worshipping cultures. She sees the cultures that worshipped goddesses as holding the key to creating a peaceful, just, egalitarian society. Although these cultures are polytheistic, in Stone's work the individual goddesses inform us about *the* Goddess of the spiritual feminist movement. This is a form of soft polytheism, where the many goddesses are aspects of one Goddess. The book's title, *When God Was a Woman,* even hints at monotheism (although this may have been an editor's choice, not Stone's). Interestingly, despite the richness with which Stone explores the ancient goddesses, the question of whether contemporary practitioners can have a relationship with them (or with a singular Goddess) is never fully addressed. *When God Was a Woman* primarily portrays Goddess religion as a tool for the political empowerment of women—a position that does not require the literal existence of a Goddess and can be embraced by nontheists.

For a slightly different feminist position, let's again consider Carol Christ's work. *She Who Changes* is consistently theistic and specifically panentheistic. In other words, the book affirms that we as human beings can have a loving relationship with Goddess/God (theism), and also that Goddess/God is fully within the world, but also more than it (panentheism). The book is less clear on the question of multiplicity. Christ seems to tip back and forth between a kind of monotheism (because "Goddess/God" is used as a singular noun) and soft polytheism (because Goddess/God has many names, and the term "Goddess/God" suggests multiplicity within unity). She never speaks of "the Goddess" and "the God," however; Christ is actively opposed to theologies that divide experience into pairs of apparent opposites, so her theology is not dualistic or duotheistic.

In this way, Christ's work starkly contrasts with that of Wiccan writers Janet and Stewart Farrar, at least as they were writing in the 1980s. The Farrars' books *The Witches' God* and *The Witches' Goddess* are excellent examples of both duotheism and theistic archetypal theology. For the Farrars, the Goddess and the God are primal creative principles that underlie all of being. At times, the Farrars seem to be simply dualists, describing the Goddess and the God as abstract "feminine and masculine essences." At other times, however, these essences are described as "ensouling" the named gods such as Isis, Pan, Demeter, and Thoth, making them "alive, real and responsive."[6] Although their metaphysical explanations of the nature of the Goddess and the God sometimes sound impersonal, in other passages the Farrars' intimate relationship with their gods is clear. In the introduction to *The Witches' Goddess,* they exhort the reader, "The Goddess is indeed real, and waiting for us to speak with her."[7] The Goddess and the God are not merely spiritual principles for the Farrars; their theology is duotheistic, not just dualistic.

The way the Farrars relate to the Goddess and the God is strongly influenced by Jungian psychology. Each book includes descriptions, myths, and rituals for the gods or goddesses of ancient pantheons. Through these gods and goddesses, the Farrars promise that the reader will be able to meet the God and Goddess of whom they are all aspects. Using a blend of psychological and metaphysical language, the Farrars describe the named deities (Isis, Pan, etc.) as "God-forms" or archetypes. They explain that archetypes are created from human thought-forms, yet give access to something that is beyond the human. The Farrars' position on whether the named gods have independent life is complex. They speak of invoking the Goddess "as Isis" or "as Aradia," suggesting that these thought-forms are like costumes that the Goddess takes on and off. They also explain that the more energy is put into these thought-forms, the more independent life they gain.[8] *The Witches' Goddess* and *The Witches' God* consistently emphasize the Two over the Many, however. The named gods, they imply, have no life without being invoked by human thought and ensouled by the Goddess and the God. This distinction sets the Farrars' work apart from that of hard polytheists, as we will see later in the chapter.

The Farrars' understanding of the Goddess and the God can be traced back to the work of ceremonial magician Aleister Crowley, who published primarily in the early to mid-twentieth century. Crowley's view differs in emphasis, however. In *Magick Without Tears,* a collection of letters that he originally wrote to a student, Crowley retells (in highly metaphysical language) the same esoteric origin story that underlies the Farrars' notion of "primal essences." In "The Universe: The 0=2 Equation,"[9] Crowley argues that behind the pairs of opposites we experience as part of reality (and that the Farrars focus on as the Goddess and the God), the essence of the universe is not a unity (monism), but rather *nothingness.* This view is not usually associated with an –ism, as "nihilism" already refers to the philosophy that life is fundamentally without meaning. One might identify this origin story, however, as one version of *creatio ex nihilo,* creation out of nothing.

Crowley's *cosmology* (his account of the origin of the universe) is influenced by Buddhism, which sees emptiness as the essential nature of being. This nothingness is not seen as negative in either Buddhism or contemporary Paganism, however. In Paganism, nothingness is a space of creative potentiality. Pagans who espouse this view tend to reject monism (the idea that the universe is of one essence) because in their eyes, the process of creation skips over unity, going directly from Nothing to Two. In the beginning, there is emptiness. Yet as soon as Something has been created, there are always already *two* things, not one: Nothing and Something, Self and Other, Perceiver and Perceived. This notion appears in various contemporary Pagan creation stories, and it is particularly beautifully told in Starhawk's *The Spiral Dance.* There, Starhawk imagines the primal nothingness as a bisexual and multiply-gendered Star Goddess who births the universe by making love to her own reflection. Her lovemaking produces a rain of bright spirits that includes the gods and, ultimately, human beings.[10]

Hard Polytheism

Hard polytheism is the view that the gods are objectively existing, independent personalities with whom human beings can have relationships. This theological position is somewhat unique in contemporary Paganism because it is the only belief around which groups of Pagans have strongly rallied. Interestingly, although conversations around hard polytheism are often framed in terms of belief, hard polytheists' objections to soft polytheism are primarily about the way belief informs practice. For hard polytheists, soft polytheist practice—especially practice that approaches the gods as interchangeable archetypes—is both less effective and potentially disrespectful. Pagans will sometimes speak of rituals where the gods do not "show up"—no energy moves, no sense of connection or presence is felt, and the participants return home in much the same mental and emotional state in which they arrived. Hard polytheists believe that this undesirable state of affairs occurs because Pagans do not recognize the nature of the gods. Hard polytheists usually experience the gods as powerful presences with distinctive desires and behaviors, as well as historical ties to particular traditions, cultures, and lands. In order to connect with a goddess or a god and form relationship with them, hard polytheists will look at rituals from the deity's native culture for guidance. When they ask a goddess or god to be present, they see themselves as calling someone very specific. Some use the metaphor of dialing a phone number to reach a friend: the ritual objects and the proper names and prayers are ways of ensuring one has the right number. Once a deity has been contacted, an ongoing relationship can be formed through prayer and ritual. This experiential relationship allows the practitioner to move beyond attempting to reconstruct an ancient religion using historical texts, and instead to create a practice that is oriented to the present.

Hard polytheists often see soft polytheists as "dialing a wrong number." Soft polytheists may treat named deities such as Aphrodite and Ishtar as if they were interchangeable—both forms of an archetypal "love goddess." To hard polytheists, this is disrespectful to the deities involved, a bit like treating two cousins as if they were the same person. A practice that does not take the deities seriously as individuals is thought to produce either weak results or none at all—or, in certain unhappy cases, a true "wrong number" where a mischievous spirit pretends to be the desired deity. Hard polytheists are also critical of soft polytheist practices that they see as self-indulgent or self-serving. Although hard polytheists do not necessarily see their deities as infallible, they regard them as sources of wisdom and inspiration who deserve devotion and service. They are concerned with the possibility that eclectic Pagans will pick and choose what appeals to them from ancient traditions while thoughtlessly rejecting anything that seems uncomfortable, or that they will make up their own traditions without being well-educated in existing ones. In their view, a soft polytheist practice may be too undisciplined to result in genuine connection with divine forces.

Hard polytheist practice contrasts strongly with the monotheism that is dominant in Western culture. As a result, hard polytheists can be actively hostile to monistic language in Paganism. Part of this may be due to a misunderstanding of monism. Hard polytheists are strongly opposed to the idea that "All gods are one God," and they tend to equate this view with monism. Yet monism does not necessarily imply a belief in a unifying personal God. Rather, it can simply indicate a belief in a unifying divine substance. Some hard polytheists do espouse ideas that are compatible with monism. Raven Kaldera is an outspoken advocate for hard polytheism in contemporary Paganism. In *Dealing with Deities*, he addresses the cross-cultural similarities between groups of gods and goddesses that some thinkers have identified as archetypes. Many polytheistic cultures, for example, have a "love goddess" of some kind. Kaldera speaks of these individual deities as sharing a divine energy current that unites them and gives them a family resemblance, while still remaining distinct personalities.[11] To draw an analogy on the human level, although a friend may be a member of a family or a citizen of a town, I don't generally think of her as "one of the Joneses" or "a Bostonian"—I think of her as "Katherine" and as an individual. Ivo Dominguez, Jr. expresses a similar idea in his book *Spirit Speak,* where he describes different levels of deity forms. For Dominguez, the named gods are also part of larger and more diffuse deity forms that unite them. Importantly, however, neither Kaldera nor Dominguez see these uniting energies as the primary focus of Pagan practice. Both take the reality of individual Pagan deities as seriously as they take the reality of individual human beings. Deities may partake in larger energies, but these writers believe that Pagans can relate to them as distinct.

For some hard polytheists, the distinction between hard and soft polytheism is primarily a difference in emphasis. In the creation myth told by Starhawk, for example, the Star Goddess gives birth to all the beings of the universe, of whom she is also part. A soft polytheist is likely to focus on the Star Goddess in this story as the common origin of all things. She may seem to be the most important deity, the oneness (or the nothingness) of which all the others are part. Yet it is not just the gods that remain a part of her, but also human beings, plants, and animals. A hard polytheist is more likely to see such a Goddess as somewhat distant and abstract, while her children—both gods and mortals—are closer to us and available for relationship. In general, hard polytheists who admit to monist underpinnings are likely to see their monism as irrelevant to their practice. The idea that there is an underlying spiritual substance to being may be an interesting metaphysical idea, but it has little impact on the everyday. (Alternatively, hard polytheists may see "divinity" as a quality shared by all deities, but deny that there is a unifying substance to being. Just as an apple and a stop sign are both "red," but not of the same substance, Aphrodite and Parvati might both be "love goddesses" and both "divine," but not of the same substance. This is a non-monist position that nevertheless affirms an essential commonality among the gods.)

Hard polytheists tend to take the issue of belief much more seriously than other Pagans. Like other Pagans, they usually emphasize that their belief in the gods is based on their personal experiences of them. However, hard polytheists see belief as a necessary part of the passion and devotion that is part of a committed relationship with the gods. As Hellenic polytheist Sarah Kate Istra Winter writes,

> I fear that paganism may not have the strength to last in the long-term if we ourselves do not firmly believe in our spiritual reality. You don't see Christians following up a discussion of accepting Jesus into your heart with some caveat like "or if you don't believe in Jesus, just imagine a similar loving entity or warm light." Or "if you need the help of a saint and don't like any of the ones you've read about, just invent a new saint in your mind that betters suits you, and contact them." As if these things are all the same. Yes, I know that many Christians go in the opposite direction and

become strictly orthodox, insisting on every detail of belief, and I also know that this is what many pagans are reacting to. But it's time to stop reacting and start building a real, solid faith that will last – and for that you need, well, *faith*.[12]

Although in this passage Winter emphasizes the necessity of belief for the Pagan movement as a whole, hard polytheist thinkers also acknowledge belief's personal dimension. Even the most devoted Pagan will not always experience the gods in all their glory; not every ritual will produce awe, ecstasy, or divine terror. In those cases, belief can help to sustain a spiritually nurturing practice. As Heathen practitioner Galina Krasskova remarked to me, "Faith and practice support me when I can't feel the gods."

Perhaps because hard polytheists are more likely to acknowledge the necessity of believing in and understanding the nature of the gods, much of the innovative contemporary Pagan theology of the past two decades has come from a hard polytheist perspective. Druid John Michael Greer's *A World Full of Gods* explores polytheism as an ethical as well as a metaphysical position. Greer spends much of his time attacking pre-twentieth century Christian theology, which may be frustrating for those who are aware that progressive Christian theology has already made these criticisms. But Greer does make a strong case for polytheism as an inherently pluralistic system in which religious tolerance and the celebration of diversity make sense. Since it is obvious from history that individuals and cultures experience the divine very differently, polytheism provides a system of thought that does not have to explain those differences away.

Other hard polytheists have focused on theoretical frameworks to support their devotional approaches, such as Northern tradition Pagan Raven Kaldera's *Dealing with Deities: Practical Polytheistic Theology*. For Kaldera, theology is not abstract or based on speculation; "faith" is a matter of trust and ongoing relationship with the gods, based on the assurance of things experienced and the conviction of things seen. He also touches on archetypal and syncretistic experiences, which have often been considered evidence for soft polytheism. Contemporary Pagans sometimes interpret similarities between deities as evidence that they have encountered a universal archetype, rather than two separate beings. These archetypal experiences seem supported by historical cases of syncretism, where deities originally from different cultures have been worshipped as the same deity. To provide a more sophisticated hard polytheist explanation for these experiences, theologian P. Sufenas Virius Lupus uses process theology and the work of polytheistic philosopher Edward P. Butler.[13] Lupus argues that deities change and evolve along with human beings, which allows new relationships to be formed among the gods over time. In turn, changes in the gods lead to changes in their relationships with humans. Lupus aims to help polytheist Pagans form deeper relationships with the gods by coming to a more consistent understanding of them.

Animism

Pagan notions of the divine are not limited to deities. Some practitioners experience plants, animals, objects, and natural phenomena such as weather as having souls or spirits. This belief is called *animism.* In contemporary Paganism, animism often overlaps with other theological positions. For instance, many hard polytheists are also animists and honor local spirits of the land as part of their practice. The spirits are understood as a different type or level of spiritual being, like the gods in some ways and distinct in others. Panentheists and soft polytheists may experience the spirits of the land as yet another aspect of a unifying divinity.

For other Pagans, however, animism is a nontheistic position. Nontheist animists do not deny a spiritual dimension to the world, and they are unlikely to see the spirits of the land as merely psychological phenomena. However, their belief and practice does not focus on deity. Some deny the existence of deity, focusing instead on the spirits of their local river or mountain, the spirits of the plants they grow in their garden, or the spirits of their local wildlife. Others acknowledge deities, but do not see them as "higher beings" or even necessarily as appropriate objects of worship. Such animists may experience deities as particularly large and complex land spirits that have limited relevance outside of their environments of origin. Rather than understanding a mountain god as an entity that can be contacted and honored regardless of location, for instance, Pagan animists may understand a mountain god as *the spirit of the mountain itself.* To Pagans who take this view, the contemporary Pagan practice of honoring gods from cultures thousands of miles away can seem nonsensical. Further, nontheist animists may not consider deities to have a special status. Animists honor all things as having living spirits; deities are just one class of non-human with whom humans can have a relationship, no more or less deserving of worship than any other living thing.

In the West, most of the innovative writing about animism is being done by writers who are not explicitly Pagan, but who have an ecological focus and experience with indigenous cultures. Religion scholar Jordan Paper's *The Deities Are Many* is both a polytheistic and an animistic book, based on Paper's fieldwork among shamanic practitioners of several cultures. Paper does not address polytheism and animism as an outside observer, however; the book expresses his personal theology, and he speaks of his sometimes rocky personal relationships with gods and spirits. David Abram's *Spell of the Sensuous* and *Becoming Animal* describe the natural environment and animals as constantly in communication with each other and, potentially, with human beings. Having spent a year living with shamanic practitioners in Bali, Abram calls on his readers to claim an essential part of the human experience by relearning how to communicate with the living earth. Finally, Graham Harvey is a scholar of animism who is explicitly Pagan. His book *Animism: Respecting the Living World* portrays animals, plants, and natural phenomena as "other-than-human persons" with whom human beings can live in reciprocal relationship. Like Abram and Paper, Harvey's theology is based on experience with living indigenous religions. None of these authors completely condemns the crowded, urban environments in which most Westerners live. All three indicate, however, that without a daily practice of communication and exchange with the natural world, connected consciousness is difficult to maintain. Action, not belief, grounds the ability to create and maintain relationships with the spirits of the land.

Experiential Theology

Christianity, and especially Protestant Christianity, tends to embrace belief for its own sake. Maintaining a belief is itself an action that connects one to the divine. Paganism differs in that belief generally follows experience rather than preceding it. There are foundational spiritual experiences that tend to orient Pagans toward particular beliefs. When these beliefs are expressed in practices, they reinforce the spiritual experience and deepen the belief (assuming, of course, that the practices are effective). For instance, some Pagans have had experiences of oneness with the world, either spontaneous or in meditation: the individual self blurs into one's surroundings, and a sense that all moments in time are simultaneously present and connected may manifest. Such Pagans tend to espouse monist, pantheist, or panentheistic beliefs and may seek out further experiences of ego loss through meditation or trance work. Other Pagans are drawn toward experiences of polarity or duality. In relationship with another being—perhaps in lovemaking—they experience a sense of two vast and primal forces coming together in a moment of ecstasy and creation. Such Pagans tend to hold dualistic or duotheistic beliefs, and they may practice rituals that explore pairs of opposites and their union. Highly personal encounters with individual gods or spirits tend to create hard polytheist Pagans, who may then court their gods as they would human lovers—giving gifts (offerings), writing poems or liturgy, and performing acts of service. Other Pagans never experience anything that might be called "supernatural" (although theist Pagans generally see their gods as entirely "natural" regardless!). These Pagans may feel moments of personal empowerment and deep joy when celebrating together in community, or find that performing rituals for a God/dess or gods makes them more effective in everyday life. Such Pagans may espouse nontheistic, psychological views of their religion.

In all these cases, the purpose of aligning oneself with a particular view of the divine is to explain experiences and motivate practice. Yet spiritual seekers may also "try on" a belief to make a particular kind of experience possible. In my own life, the desire for a more intense, more intimate, and more personal practice motivated my own shift from a mystical Christianity that honored God/dess by many names, to a soft polytheist Paganism that saw the one beyond the many, to a more-or-less hard polytheist practice that still acknowledges a unifying divine current. For me, a hard polytheist approach to the gods has granted me the personal relationships, the awesome beauty, and the holy terror that I longed for. But if these practices had not produced valuable experiences—in other words, if the experiment had failed—the new beliefs and practices surely would have fallen away. In contemporary Paganism, we do not see belief detached from practice as worthwhile by itself.

So many of us are seeking meaning, seeking divinity, seeking the gods. I invite the reader to engage the deities, the Deity, or the divine as part of an ongoing process of experimentation and discovery. May we find that which we seek, and also discover more than we could have imagined.

Summary

Pagan beliefs about deities and the divine are complex, with practitioners often holding more than one view at once, or holding different views depending on context. Belief tends to arise out of personal experience rather than preceding it, and it is solidified by repeated spiritual experiences achieved through practice. Pagan views of deity emphasize immanence, or the presence of the divine in the physical world. Some Pagans experience the divine as ultimately unified, as in pantheist, panentheist, monist, and soft polytheist views. These views are expressed frequently in feminist Pagan theology. Other Pagans tend to see the world as consisting of two underlying primal forces (dualism or duotheism), a view that is common in British Wicca and related traditions. Much of the theological innovation occurring in contemporary Paganism today is coming from self-identified hard polytheists, who either reject the idea of a unifying divinity or see it as irrelevant. The hard polytheist view is related to animism, which sees all things as having a living spirit. Many animists are not explicitly Pagan, but are instead informed by indigenous religions and ecological theology. The animistic notion of reciprocity, where relationships between humans and other-than-human persons require exchange, is having a strong influence on contemporary Pagan theology, especially on hard polytheists.

Activities

Reflect on your beliefs in a journal. What theological positions do you identify with? What theology is expressed by your religious practice? Have your beliefs changed over the course of your life, or do they change based on context? Think back to childhood or young adulthood. Was there any powerful spiritual experience that led you to your religion? How do you seek spiritual experiences now?

What would it be like to honor the divine differently? Consider experimenting with a practice that is different from the beliefs that you hold. Can a hard polytheist meditate on Atman (the soul of the universe) with a group of Hindus? Can a monotheist make offerings to the spirits of the land, understanding them as aspects of the divine? Can a soft polytheist or nontheist call upon a deity and speak to him or her as a person, rather than an archetype? Sit with the feelings of discomfort that may arise from this thought experiment. Is it important to continue to believe as you do now? Why or why not?

Further Reading

Bridger, Margarian. "Pagan Deism: Three Views." *The Pomegranate: A New Journal of NeoPagan Thought* 1:1 (1997). 37-42. Available at http://proteuscoven.com/triangle.htm.

Butler, Edward P. *Essays on a Polytheistic Philosophy of Religion.* New York City: Phaidra Editions, 2012.

Cleary, Collin. *Summoning the Gods.* San Francisco, CA: Counter-Currents Publishing, 2011.

Goddess Thealogy: An International Journal for the Study of the Divine Feminine, Vol. 1 No. 1 (December 2011). Available at http://glasgow.academia.edu/PatriciaIolana/Books/1260406/G oddess_Thealogy_An_International_Journal_for_the_Study_of_the _Divine_Feminine_Vol_1_No._1_December_2011.

Starhawk. *The Spiral Dance.* 20th Anniversary Edition. San Francisco: Harper San Francisco, 1999 (1979). Chapters 5 and 6.

Winter, Sarah Kate Istra. *Kharis: Hellenic Polytheism Explored.* CreateSpace, 2008.

Chapter Two

Myth, Tradition, and Innovation

The foundation of contemporary Pagan theology is myth.
Given the colloquial use of the word "myth," this statement may sound a bit strange. In Western culture, "myth" often means "a prevalent belief that isn't true" (as in the popular television show *Mythbusters,* which tests common beliefs about the world with the scientific method). We also commonly speak of "mythology" when referring to stories of the goddesses, gods, and heroes of ancient cultures. This usage comes closer to the way "myth" is understood in contemporary Paganism, but it's still somewhat off the mark. In mainstream society, myths are often taught as the quaint productions of premodern civilizations, with the understanding that if myths are still told in a modern context, they are preserved as part of cultural or ethnic heritage or, at most, because they convey important psychological truths. Contemporary Paganism, on the other hand, takes myths seriously as sacred stories that express values and suggest modes of behavior.

Some Pagans agree with comparative religion scholar Joseph Campbell, who presented myths as guiding individuals through stages of life and expressing truths that are universal to the human condition. Others experience myths as offering access to numinous powers and beings with whom seekers can develop relationships. Although myths may appear to refer to a time in the distant past, they are often better understood as occurring in an eternal present, sometimes repeating over and over as part of a recurring cycle (for example, the Wiccan seasonal cycle known as the "Wheel of the Year"). Pagans often look to the myths of pre-Christian religious traditions (such as stories of Greek, Egyptian, Celtic, and Norse deities) and to those of living indigenous traditions for inspiration. Such traditions are often seen as having a more authentic connection to the earth, a particular piece of land, a people, or the divine. Other Pagans approach the religious myths of their childhood from a Pagan perspective, or create new sacred tales that, over time, begin to function as myths in their communities.

Pagans delight in narrative in general, and a story need not be old or from a foreign country to offer spiritual inspiration. When American religion scholar Sarah Pike studied Pagan festivals, she found that many Pagans located the beginnings of their spirituality in the fantasy or science fiction that they first read as children or young adults.[1] Speculative fiction of this kind tends to be idea-driven and to offer modes of behavior and relationship that are different from the mainstream. Fiction allows Pagans to imagine alternatives ways of relating to the land, to the divine, and to each other. One significant contemporary Pagan group, the Church of All Worlds, took its name directly from *Stranger in a Strange Land,* an influential science fiction novel by Robert Heinlein. The group's emphasis on close personal bonding and sexual freedom reflects the values of the fictional religion that Heinlein imagined. In turn, the real-life Church of All Worlds has advocated for those values through the magazine *Green Egg,* which had a huge impact on the infant American Pagan movement of the 1970s.[2] Pagans have also used fiction to spread their beliefs and practices throughout the Pagan community and beyond. Starhawk's novel *The Fifth Sacred Thing,* for example, presents many of the practices of her real-life Reclaiming community as part of a futuristic dystopian narrative.

Narrative plays an important role in many of the world's religions. Among Jews, the story of the Exodus is retold yearly at Passover as they imagine an era of peace and justice and a return to Jerusalem. Buddhists use jataka tales—stories of the Buddha's many lives—to teach morality, as do Christians with stories of Jesus, the apostles, or the saints. Similarly, Native American stories of ancestors and animal spirits teach tribal values and traditions, as well as orienting listeners to the land on which they live. Pagans differ somewhat from these other religions in that they usually do not limit themselves to a single body of literature or tradition. There are some exceptions to this, particularly among those reconstructing ancient religions from historical texts and archeological study, but the majority of Pagans are at least somewhat eclectic. This tendency reflects Pagans' emphasis on having a religious practice that feels personally meaningful, as well as their resistance to anything that smacks of dogmatism. The meaning of sacred stories is never fully fixed; story *requires* interpretation. Individual practitioners are often encouraged to feel out the meaning of a myth for themselves, and to seek the experiential truth—the *mystery*—at the heart of the tale.

Not all Pagans feel comfortable picking and choosing from many cultures, however. Some self-impose restrictions on their choice of material, feeling that completely unrestricted eclecticism lacks sufficient structure. To attempt to deepen their connection to a particular place, culture, deity, or group, Pagans will sometimes limit themselves to working with the myths of a single culture or the liturgical materials of a single Pagan tradition. Others are concerned with cultural appropriation, and they disapprove of taking stories and practices from other cultures out of their intended context. In those cases, Pagans may focus their work on the religious traditions of their ancestors, or on the traditions of communities with whom they have a meaningful relationship. Special care must be taken when approaching indigenous or minority religious communities who have been historically oppressed and may still be experiencing economic, social, and legal disadvantages. For example, because of the genocidal history between Native Americans and white settlers, non-Native Pagans seeking training in Native religion must be sensitive to the concerns of traditional practitioners. While a sincere seeker who wants to contribute to the well-being of Native communities may be tentatively welcomed, some Native American peoples see whites as commodifying their spirituality and attempting to strip-mine their religion for exotic tidbits. Pagans seeking to become part of Native communities must first develop a basis for mutual trust.

Pagans employ myths in both collective and individual contexts. Myths form the basis of many group rituals. In Wicca, for example, practitioners celebrate the Wheel of the Year, which links the story of the dying and rising God and the Goddess who appears as Maiden, Mother, and Crone into the seasonal cycle. Birth, death, and fertility are celebrated in response to the waxing and waning sun and the cycle of planting, growth, harvest, and fallowness. Some groups put on ritual dramas to tell the seasonally linked tales of the gods, such as the myth of Persephone. In this myth, the seasons are related to the grief and celebration of Persephone's mother Demeter. Demeter allows the earth to grow when Persephone returns from the underworld each year, but grieves and blights the land when her daughter descends to her husband Hades, lord of the dead. Such rituals help to connect participants with larger natural forces or with the gods themselves.

Individuals may also use myths to define their identities, create meaning around life events, or recover from trauma. Feminist Paganism has often used goddess myths for personal empowerment; women and men are encouraged to bring the virtues of various goddesses into their lives by telling their stories, honoring them in worship, and imitating their strengths. A woman seeking to become more independent in her life, for instance, might build an altar to Diana or Artemis and take up archery as a hobby while also applying for a promotion at her job.

Myths can also help individuals to turn adversity or trauma into spiritual growth. The popular myth of Inanna—another story of descent to the underworld—tells the harrowing tale of the goddess's journey below, where she is systematically stripped of her symbols of power, then slain and hung as a naked corpse by her dark sister, Ereshkigal. But Inanna has planned ahead for the risky journey, and after three days and nights, her allies bargain with Ereshkigal, recover Inanna's body, and return her to life. Inanna must send another to the underworld in her place, however. When she returns to the surface and finds that her husband Dumuzi is not mourning her death, she chooses him to replace her in the land of the dead.

Many individuals have used the myth of Inanna to deal with experiences of trauma, particularly trauma that resulted from voluntary actions. Ereshkigal is sometimes experienced as a stern taskmaster who oversees an ultimately transformative ordeal, and parallels can be drawn between Inanna's resurrection and that of Jesus. Unlike in the Christian tradition, where scriptural stories are often read for ethical lessons, Pagans read myths as offering spiritual insight, not directly prescribing behavior. In the myth of Inanna, it is possible to read Inanna's punishment of Dumuzi as "rightful revenge." But contemporary Pagans may instead see it as a warning not to lash out against loved ones who do not understand the ordeal they have undergone. Common Pagan interpretations of the myth also include the transformative potential of vulnerability and the greater strength that can be built from having survived powerlessness.[3]

Although Pagans do sometimes imitate their gods, as in the example of a woman devoting herself to Artemis in her quest for independence, gods are usually held up as exemplars of specific virtues rather than paragons of ethical behavior. As scholar Graham Harvey remarks about contemporary Heathenry, "Northern religion, Paganism, and other polytheistic traditions in general find meaning and value in the diverse ordinary lives of human beings. The deities *introduce us to ourselves* and do not only demand allegiance and worship" [my emphasis].[4] Relationships with deity lead practitioners into deeper relationship with their humanity, rather than with a transcendent moral law. Although there is a certain amount of playful mockery around the issue of the gods and their ethics (for example, the bumper sticker "WWTD: What Would Thor Do?"), the gods are thought to hold great but context-specific wisdom. The fact that most Pagans honor multiple gods (either as individual personalities, or as aspects of a God/dess or a Goddess and a God) is consistent with contemporary Pagan virtue ethics, which stresses the cultivation of many virtues in a harmonious balance. A devotee of the Greek gods might honor Aphrodite as a goddess of beauty and sexual love, but Aphrodite lacks the virtues of fidelity and constancy. For a successful marriage or a harmonious household, Pagans might turn to Hera, who presides over weddings, or Hestia, goddess of the hearth. Even the ancient Greeks were sometimes critical of their gods, who could be petty and capricious; yet the imperfect gods still had their devotees, and their worship was at the center of a stable culture for hundreds of years. Contemporary Pagans seek to learn spiritual lessons from their myths, while nevertheless employing the sophisticated ethical thinking of Western philosophy. Some might even assert that human ethics—ethics that grow from being embodied and finite on the earth—are one of the gifts that Pagans offer back to their gods, whose perspective is not bound by a human sense of space or time.

Myth vs. History: Myths of Pagan Origins

Sociologist Kenneth Rees has been studying contemporary Pagans and their uses of myth since the 1970s. He describes myths as stories that define identity, teach us about the world, and help to organize human behavior. According to Rees, important myths often operate covertly in the Pagan community under the label of "history."[5] Such myths may be based on historical or scientific fact, but they are necessarily an interpretation of those facts. When myths are labeled as "history," however, many people lose sight of their interpretive, subjective quality.

Some of these myths overlap with myths of American culture. Consider, for example, the *myth of progress*—the belief that through technology, cultural advances, scientific discoveries, and more, the human species is evolving towards an ever higher and better form. In the United States, the myth of progress often goes hand in hand with millennialism, or the belief in a coming age of peace and prosperity (sometimes associated with the Second Coming of Christ, the new Age of Aquarius, or both). Pagans and other Americans alike often read evolutionary theory through the myth of progress, believing that there is an emergent purpose to natural selection that inevitably produces beings of greater beauty, sophistication, and power. Yet this myth of progress wars with the competing *myth of decline*, which looks back to a lost Golden Age of righteousness and justice and fears the coming of a catastrophic apocalypse. (Whether this apocalypse comes at the hand of an angry God or an abused earth varies.) Our current historical moment provides some of the "facts" for both of these myths, but neither myth is provable. Both are interpretations of historical patterns that are still in motion.

Druid John Michael Greer is critical of the confusion of myth and history in the contemporary Pagan community, particularly in the United States. This is a confusion that exists elsewhere in American culture, however. Biblical scholars have sometimes experienced the ire of practicing Christians when the historical study of the Bible seemed to undermine its status as a literal account. Historical evidence of a global flood, or of the enslavement of the Israelites in Egypt, is celebrated; evidence against these events is attacked as a politically or religiously motivated attempt to undermine Christianity. Believing that the legitimacy of their religion rests on a particular version of history, some contemporary Pagans also suffer from this attachment to certain versions of history. Yet history is interpretive; multiple narratives of the facts are always possible. Greer writes:

> The common notion that history is simply "what happened" is naïve, to use no harsher word; "what happened" in any single day in any small town, recorded in detail, would fill volumes. The historian must select—must decide what is important and what is not—and makes the selection, consciously or not, on the basis of the story he or she is trying to tell.

History, however, is not purely subjective, nor is it the same as myth:

> Historians are indeed in the business of storytelling, but the stories they tell are bound by a set of very specific rules, foremost among them the rule that every event in their stories should be a verifiable fact. [... History's] purpose is to show the texture and flow of past events, in all their complexity and ambiguity[....] This purpose can overlap to some degree with the goals of myth (or of fiction), but overlap is not the same as identity.[6]

Greer suggests that Americans tend to make two errors. First, they read history as established, incontrovertible truth, rather than as theory in process. And second, they attempt to use history as myth—in other words, as a narrative intended to create and sustain meaning in communities. As a result, says Greer, we fail to criticize these meaning-making narratives: we do not ask what the myths are teaching us or what kind of society they are leading us to create. "Not all myths," he states flatly, "are constructive, positive, or useful."[7]

Two historically-based myths that have strongly influenced contemporary Paganism are the *myth of matriarchal prehistory* and the *myth of the Burning Times*. Both are narratives of Pagan origins, and both are based on scholarly research. Unfortunately, these narratives primarily draw on scholarship that is decades old. Pagans have become attached to these versions of history and sometimes feel threatened when new research calls them into question. Scholars seeking to replace these historical narratives with new ones are sometimes perceived as attacking the Pagan community itself—and it is true that scholarly arguments are sometimes politically motivated. At other times, however, scholars who are sympathetic to Paganism or who are Pagan themselves still find that their research contradicts certain Pagan beliefs. Despite the emphasis on practice and experience as the fundamental bases for contemporary Paganism, Pagans (like other American religious people) sometimes cling fiercely to particular interpretations of texts. While for some Christians, the text that cannot be questioned is the Bible, for Pagans the texts are archeological and anthropological studies.

The myth of matriarchal prehistory is an ongoing site of controversy, especially among feminist Pagans and Goddess-worshippers. The narrative is largely based on the research of Marija Gimbutas, a Lithuanian-American archeologist who did groundbreaking work on Neolithic Europe. Her studies of figurines from this period—showing a variety of female, male, and animal-human hybrid forms—contributed enormously to our knowledge about Neolithic civilization. Unfortunately, the conclusions that Gimbutas drew from her data were overly broad. Although her illustrations make it easy to believe that Neolithic Europeans worshipped goddesses, Gimbutas speaks most often of "the Goddess," suggesting a monotheism that doesn't seem to fit the enormous variety of representations. Further, Gimbutas argued that this Goddess-worshipping culture was pacifistic, egalitarian and led by priestesses, but that it was destroyed when the patriarchal Kurgans invaded from what is now Russia. Yet subsequent research has uncovered weapons, bodies showing evidence of wounding by projectiles, and fortifications that precede the date Gimbutas gives for the arrival of the Kurgans. Although unusually egalitarian societies that worshipped goddesses as well as gods may have existed in the Neolithic era, the utopian matriarchy that Gimbutas describes probably did not.[8]

Some Pagans and spiritual feminists have chosen to use the myth of matriarchal prehistory as an inspirational sacred story, rather than understanding it as pure history. In this way, the story has supported activists in working for a more peaceful and more egalitarian society. By imagining a just society that might once have existed, feminist Pagans and Goddess-worshippers galvanize themselves to try to create such a society in the present day. Other Pagans, however, have been critical of the matriarchal myth. Greer, for instance, notes that the myth of matriarchal prehistory has many similarities to the story of the Garden of Eden.[9] In the story from Genesis, humankind falls from grace and is cast out of utopia because of Eve's disobedience. In Christianity, Eve's "sin" has sometimes been blamed on women in general, and the Genesis story has been used to discriminate against women. The matriarchal myth reverses this sexism by envisioning a female-led utopia that was destroyed by "patriarchal invaders"—in other words, by men. Although both the matriarchal myth and the myth of the Garden of Eden can be interpreted in a non-sexist fashion, both narratives have been used to teach gender-based prejudice.

A second myth of Pagan origins is the narrative of the Burning Times. Based on the research of British anthropologist Margaret Murray, this narrative argues that the witch hunts of medieval and Renaissance Europe targeted practitioners of an ancient, indigenous Western European religion. The "witches" who were persecuted by the Inquisition of the Catholic Church were not simply Christian heretics, but rather the priestesses and priests of a religion with an unbroken lineage back to ancient times. According to Murray and other scholars' research, most of the victims of these witch hunts were female, and many were practitioners of folk healing arts. When Gerald Gardner first began to publicize Wicca (now the largest contemporary Pagan tradition) in the 1950s, he drew directly on Murray's research when he claimed to have discovered and been initiated into one of the last remaining covens of this ancient religion. Pagans and feminists came to see these "witches" as martyrs, both for a Goddess-worshipping religion and for women.

Scholars initially believed that as many as nine million people had been murdered over several centuries of persecution. Subsequent research, however, has decreased these numbers substantially to some hundreds of thousands. Additionally, Murray's argument for the unbroken survival of an ancient religion has not held up well to scrutiny.[10] While it is true that many aspects of contemporary Wicca have ancient roots, it seems likely that they did not pass to us from ancient times in a single package. Aspects of ancient theology survived in art and literature; rituals and healing practices survived as folk magic; and indigenous holy days survived as seasonal festivals, often Christianized. It seems clear that magickal and occult practices were present during the medieval period, and also that the myths and legends of the ancient gods continued to be told (sometimes as stories of saints). However, the underground religion on a mass scale that Murray imagined in Western Europe likely did not exist.

The Burning Times narrative continues to hold currency in contemporary Paganism, however. Scholar Chris Klassen has pointed out that both the myth of the Burning Times and the myth of matriarchal prehistory allow contemporary Pagans to identify with a persecuted group. These narratives can help to explain and justify Pagans' countercultural status or sense of being different from the mainstream. Stories of persecution can also help Pagans find solidarity with other minority groups. On the other hand, as Klassen points out, most Pagans are white and relatively economically privileged. Identifying with persecuted witches or Goddess-worshippers might be counterproductive if it encourages Pagans not to take responsibility for their part in perpetuating an unjust society.[11]

A third myth of Pagan origins is one that is particularly dear to my heart, and yet it is equally questionable as a literal, historical tale: the *myth of Paganism as a root religion*. In this narrative, the first religion of humanity is imagined as a religion of the earth and of the human body, with devotion offered to the many numinous beings that humans experienced in the world around them. Problems arise, however, when scholars and Pagans attempt to define exactly what this primal religion consisted of. Many scholars have attempted to "discover" the primal religion by looking for its remnants in the world's religions, and particularly in the indigenous religions that have survived into the modern period. Unfortunately, while such scholars often produce fascinating studies comparing the religions of the world, their reasoning is circular. It is all too easy to choose elements from the world's religions that one finds particularly attractive and then—because the religions of the world are enormously diverse—to find those elements buried in nearly every religious culture. Greer makes this argument against Paul Ingram's notion of a "primordial tradition,"[12] and one could similarly critique the philosophical notion of "perennialism," the idea that particular metaphysical truths arise in every culture.

The problem is not so much the idea that some truths are universal to humanity; rather, the problem is in the process of deciding exactly what those truths are. During the period when religious studies was dominated by scholars who were also Christian clergy, for example, "universal truths" tended to be equated with the truths found in Christianity. Scholars would then find "precursors" of those Christian truths in other religions. The world's other religions, in other words, were seen either as necessary steps toward the creation of a superior Christian faith, or as flawed variations of that faith. Those who argue for Paganism as the root religion are using this strategy in reverse. Nineteenth-century Christian scholars saw Christianity as one of the last faiths to emerge, and the fact that it was last was proof that it was the best. Pagans who portray Paganism as the root religion tend to make the opposite argument, that because Paganism was first, it is the superior basis for all other religions. The question of whether contemporary Paganism significantly resembles ancient religions, let alone the primal religion of the human race, is rarely effectively answered.

Scholar Michael York presents one of the better versions of the "root religion" narrative in *Pagan Theology*. Rather than making a historical argument for a root religion, York instead wants to present paganism (with a small "p") as one of four valid, global religious perspectives. He sets up a system of four religious positions: the Abrahamic, the dharmic, the secular, and the pagan. York's four religious positions cut across traditions. Although each position is particularly strong in specific religious traditions (for instance, most Jews, Muslims, and Christians hold Abrahamic attitudes, and most Buddhists and Hindus hold dharmic ones), there are Hindus who hold the pagan position, Jews who hold the secular position, and more. York sees the "pagan" position reflected in all the world's religious traditions, though most especially in indigenous ones. For York, paganism includes multiple deities, the perception that all living things have souls or spirits, the use of images or "idols" in worship, a spirituality that relates to the body or the material, an emphasis on locale and on sacred aspects of geography, and nature worship of some kind.[13] He suggests that these factors appear in so many of the world's religions because they represent human beings' first religious impulses.

Being a contemporary Pagan, I find much of what York has to say to be compelling. It does seem to me that whatever humanity's first religious impulses were, they must have sprung from the realities of the human body and its experiences of eating, sleeping, hunting, gathering, and relating to other beings. But we are no longer hunter-gatherers, nor are we even the same species as the first beings in Africa who might have been called "human."[14] What humanity's first religious impulses were is pure speculation. Additionally, the choice of the word "pagan" to describe this primal religious impulse is problematic because the word has become so strongly identified with the contemporary Pagan movement. With an estimated 1.2 million self-identifying Pagans in the United States alone,[15] and significant numbers of contemporary Pagans in the UK, Australia, and elsewhere, Paganism is rapidly growing in urban environments. It is a relatively affluent movement of Westerners who aspire to the intimate consciousness that (many of us believe) comes from living in deep connection with a place and/or with one's ancestors. This consciousness is still a reality in indigenous societies, but many contemporary Pagans are trying to fumble their way back to this kind of knowing without so much as a road map. David Abram, writing of his time studying with the shamanic practitioners of Bali, mourns that his sense of intense presence to the living world started to slip within a few weeks of returning to an urban American environment. Rather than experiencing water, wind, animals, birds, insects, and plants as vibrantly alive and constantly communicating with each other and with him, Abram found himself returning to a consciousness where the world no longer spoke.[16] Abram is careful not to denigrate the accomplishments of our highly technological society, but he—like most Pagans— longs to recover and retain what he believes is a primal human consciousness.

In this, both York and Abram see indigenous peoples as potential resources and allies. Yet indigenous people do not necessarily see contemporary Pagans in the same light. Firstly, they are unlikely to claim the term "pagan," as the word has a long history of derogatory use in the West. Indigenous spokespeople from around the world are instead using "Indigenous" as the umbrella term for cultures and religions that are place-based. In a significant 2009 statement at A Parliament of World's Religions, a group speaking on behalf of "Indigenous Peoples" pointed out the threat that environmental changes present to their way of life. The statement called on the Pope and the Catholic Church to repudiate the Doctrine of Discovery and Dominion, which they see as having justified colonization and the stripping of natural resources by Westerners.[17]

It is presumptuous, to say the least, for contemporary Pagans to lay claim to the religions of indigenous people by calling them "pagan." Sadly, most Pagans are deeply embedded in Western culture, with its tendencies to abuse both minority groups and the earth's resources in order to consolidate wealth and power. Although some indigenous people are willing to accept contemporary Pagans as allies, others see them as exploitative. Pagan practitioner Andras Corban Arthen has traveled around Europe seeking groups who may still be practicing indigenous European religious traditions. Such religious practices (preserved as "folk traditions") have remained strong in certain areas of Lithuania and have drawn interest from scholars.[18] In a lecture, Arthen related his slow process of befriending practitioners of native Lithuanian religion, and he spoke of their suspicion of contemporary Pagans and New Age practitioners. Fearing that contemporary Pagans will take their religion out of context, Arthen said, some of the older Lithuanians expressed that they would rather have their traditions die out than to see them commodified by contemporary Pagans.[19] Such expectations are barriers to interfaith understanding between Pagans and indigenous practitioners.

Although the notion that contemporary Paganism is a throwback to root religion is appealing, this is a myth that needs to be employed carefully. In attempting to recreate a primal religion, contemporary Pagans must respect the indigenous peoples that inspire them, and they must take indigenous political concerns seriously. As with the myths of matriarchal prehistory and the Burning Times, the myth of Paganism as a root religion has historical aspects. Historical accounts, however, should not be the primary source of legitimacy for Pagans. Encouraging Pagans to look to the present and to their real life environments, Pagan theologian Starhawk wrote an article titled "Religion from Nature, Not from Archaeology."[20] I would alter that slightly to say "Religion from Experience"—for Pagan theology is strongest when based on our collective and individual experiences, not just of nature, but also of our own bodies and minds. Though we often think of ourselves as being separate from our environment, we are an integral part of its complex organic system. The attempt to regain our connectedness with the world is the strength of contemporary Paganism, not a speculative connection to particular versions of history.

Authenticity

Many Pagans are anxious about whether their practices are *authentic*. Particularly in North America, there is tension around whether legitimacy comes from tradition—from the practice of doing something over and over and passing it down through the generations—or from innovation, where practices respond to the present and look toward the future. Those who think that innovation is inherently authentic often choose their religious practices by saying, "If it works for me, then it's the right thing." I agree that innovation is important in religion, lest our practices become rote and passionless. On the other hand, judging practices purely on whether they "work" for an individual gives little protection against the human tendency to fall prey to personal biases. Established religious traditions have tools to challenge practitioners and create spiritual growth. When we pick and choose an eclectic path with no guidance from elders or established tradition, we risk creating religious practices that are personally and spiritually stagnant. It's out of a fear of this kind of weak eclecticism that some Pagans fasten so fervently on historical traditions, as these established practices (even if half-forgotten) promise a connection to cultures and ways of being that may have much to teach us in the present.

Pagans often look to indigenous cultures (as well as historical records of indigenous cultures) in the hope of recovering an originally oral current of authentic religious knowledge. Widespread misunderstanding about how oral cultures transmit their knowledge, however, can lead Pagans to dogmatic interpretations of folklore. Literate Westerners tend to imagine that oral cultures pass down information word for word, unchanging, and that is how tradition is preserved. But as professional folklorists know, knowledge in oral cultures is constantly in process. Whenever stories are shared, they are being performed for a specific audience. The performer shapes the tales to the people who are present in the moment. The continuity of folklore is created both by the material itself, which each storyteller receives from his or her predecessors, and also by the container of the community in which the stories are told. It is not just the lore, but also the community, that creates an unbroken thread of transmission. In these traditional societies, innovation and tradition go hand in hand. An "authentic" tale from an oral culture requires both aspects. One might say that writing down these stories, removing them from community and freezing them in time on a page, is actually the best way to render them *in*authentic.[21]

The most exciting trends in contemporary Paganism involve groups that take their study of history and comparative religion seriously while not being too attached to any particular version of "the way things were." To cling too tenaciously to a historical account limits practitioners' ability to move into the experiential, performative space where ritual and story come alive, where broken traditions become living ones once again. I myself am particularly fond of Pagans' use of myth to engage new scientific knowledge. Because scientific knowledge, like historical knowledge, is a set of ever-evolving theories based on known facts, couplings of science and myth must be loose to be successful. Yet the enthusiasm of Pagans for finding mythic truths in scientific theory is one of the ways that Paganism puts itself in harmony with science. Pagans are able to embrace new scientific knowledge and work in scientific fields, without having to choose between religious community and the opportunity to move human knowledge forward. For example, Pagans have been delighted by the Gaia hypothesis put forward by James Lovelock and Lynn Margulis. This theory suggests that all of the Earth's organisms and inorganic matter work together as a single self-regulating, interdependent system that maintains the conditions for life to exist. The Gaia hypothesis offers a new framework that contextualizes and connects various scientific disciplines. Many Pagans have embraced it as a way to think about pantheism, the idea that all things are God/dess. The notion of the earth as a complex system helps Pagans think concretely about interdependence.

As with historical narratives, Pagans must be careful not to understand scientific theories as unchanging, objective truth; as science evolves, so must Pagans' understanding of its mythic dimensions. Neither can they uncritically embrace pseudoscientific theories that promise to justify their theology. As with all theories, new scientific ideas must be tested by experimentation and must hold up over time. Nevertheless, Pagans' positive interaction with science is a strength, especially in an American religious culture where religion and science are often thought to be opposed.

Summary

Contemporary Pagan theology cannot exist apart from myth and narrative. As in all religious traditions, myths are the foundation of Pagans' understanding of who they are and the world they live in. Pagans, however, engage in interpretation of myth in an active, conscious way. They frequently reinterpret both ancient and contemporary narratives for the purposes of individual and collective spiritual exploration. Pagans sometimes conflate myth with history and find themselves problematically attached to debunked scholarship. They also struggle to think critically about the myths they choose to embrace and how to interpret them, since not all myths will support healthy spiritual growth or a just society. Because of the Western heritage of colonization and exploitation of natural resources, Pagans must proceed delicately when engaging indigenous practitioners as sources of myth and tradition. In general, Pagans are able to use traditional myths in innovative ways, but they are also actively creating new sacred stories of their own, especially myths based on new scientific narratives.

Activities

Read a book of mythology. (One you loved as a child is particularly good.) Find a myth that speaks to you. What does this myth tell you about the people from whom it came? How did they see themselves? Where did they come from? What was their place in the universe or their purpose in being?

Spend time thinking about this myth in the context of your own life. What about this myth speaks to you here and now? Does it remind you of events in your life, or does it capture your hopes or fears?

Try meditating on this myth daily, ten minutes a day, for one week. Record your thoughts in a journal. What deeper meanings might this myth hold for you?

Further Reading

Rees, Kenneth. "The Tangled Skein: The Role of Myth in Paganism." *Paganism Today*. Ed. Graham Harvey and Charlotte Hardman. London: Thorsons, 1996, 16-31.

Campbell, Joseph. *The Power of Myth*. New York: Anchor Books, 1988.

Kraemer, Christine Hoff. "Cultural Borrowing/Cultural Appropriation: A Relationship Model for Respectful Borrowing." *Thorn Magazine* 2 (Mar 2009): 36-39. Available at http://cherryhillseminary.academia.edu/ChristineKraemer/Papers/1175646/Cultural_Borrowing_Cultural_Appropriation_A_Relationship_Model_for_Respectful_Borrowing.

-----. "Perceptions of Scholarship in Contemporary Paganism." American Academy of Religion Annual Conference, San Francisco, CA, 19-22 Nov 2011. Available at http://cherryhillseminary.academia.edu/ChristineKraemer/Talks/64074/Perceptions_of_Scholarship_in_Contemporary_Paganism.

-----. "'Story' Is Only Part of 'History': Re-evaluating the Work of Marija Gimbutas." *Thorn Magazine* 1 (Dec 2008): 48-52. Available at http://cherryhillseminary.academia.edu/ChristineKraemer/Papers/1175643/Story_Is_Only_Part_of_History_Re-evaluating_the_Work_of_Marija_Gimbutas.

Chapter Three

Knowledge and Devotion

Through personal experience, Pagans seek divine knowledge to inform their devotional practices.

I once read a remarkably accurate booklet about contemporary Paganism from an evangelical Christian. The author did an impressive job of summarizing the history of the movement, naming key figures in its development, and describing contemporary Pagan theology's emphasis on intuition and individual experience. He made what I thought were legitimate criticisms at that point—if personal experience is the primary basis for belief and practice, how do individuals and groups deal with a person whose beliefs are a product of mental illness? Even more importantly, if all personal religious experience is legitimate, how does a group make ethical distinctions? If a person believes that the gods are instructing him to exploit or abuse another person, on what basis can others declare that he is wrong? Having personal experience as the basis for one's theology can look scarily like having no standards at all. I had to laugh, though, when the pamphlet writer suggested trying to convert Pagans to Christianity by showing them passages from the Bible. For that writer, biblical text was an authoritative standard on which to base his religion. But what led him to accept the Bible as a legitimate authority? Was it family or community tradition? Reasoned arguments that convinced him the book must be the literal word of God? Or did he have an experience of being born again through Jesus Christ?

Ultimately, I felt, this evangelical writer was not so different from the Pagans he criticized. Religious authority is *always* accepted through personal experience. The experience of being raised in a loving community of religious practitioners leads many people to embrace that religion as their own. The experience of being intellectually persuaded by logical arguments and historical facts leads others to convert to a new religion or leave their old one (and significantly, not everyone is convinced by the same arguments, nor does everyone agree that the "right" religion is the most logical one). And finally, the experience of hearing, seeing, or sensing a divine presence is part of the personal narratives of many deeply religious people, both Christian and Pagan. Somewhere in every religious person's life there has been a leap of faith, however much evidence may also have been involved—a leap of faith that one's community, one's chosen book of scripture, one's reason, or one's intuition is trustworthy.

So when I say that Pagans rely primarily on personal experience for their theology, I do not mean necessarily that every Pagan has mystical visions or uncanny intuitions (although some Pagans do, at least some of the time). Rather, I mean that when it comes to religious authority, Pagans know that the buck stops with them. No institution or book, promising reliability and legitimacy, stands between Pagans and the divine (with a few exceptions, as we'll see later). More than in many of the world's religions, Pagans are aware that they are discovering their own spirituality, and they are directly responsible for their own successes and mistakes. This is the meaning behind the Wiccan principle that every practitioner is her own priest/ess. Clearly, not every Pagan is a priest/ess in the sense that she is a trained ritualist, counselor, magick worker, seer, and group leader. Rather, it means that no mediator is necessary between Pagans and their gods.

Evaluating Religious Experience

The study of knowledge—in other words, how we know what we know—is called *epistemology*. Contemporary Paganism does not have a formal epistemology, but Pagans do think and write a great deal about the nature of knowing: firstly, about how practitioners can gain information about human/divine relationships, and secondly, about the process of integrating such information into a broader context, converting it into usable knowledge. The broader context for knowledge often involves group structures, such as traditions or communities. As in other religions, Pagans' belief has a social aspect; Pagans' sense of what is known is shaped by the beliefs of others in their communities, whether in person or online. The pressure to conform to a Pagan group's beliefs tends to be weaker than in mainstream religions, however. While becoming part of a Pagan group may help a new practitioner to make like-minded friends, Pagan groups rarely provide a platform for success in business or local politics the way mainstream churches and synagogues can—especially since it is not only acceptable, but common for Pagans to practice on their own. This is one of many reasons that Pagan religious experiences tend to be so individual.

In the influential book *The Varieties of Religious Experience,* psychologist William James suggests a basis for judging religious experience. James argues that religious experiences are universal to human beings and legitimate regardless of their origins (whether they are connected to some external divine being, or simply products of the human mind). He proposes that religious experiences should be evaluated by their results, using the criteria of *immediate luminousness, philosophical reasonableness,* and *moral helpfulness.* The criterion of "luminousness" differentiates a religious experience from one that is merely pleasurable: getting drunk isn't a religious experience in itself, but having an experience of oneness with the land while dancing and intoxicated might be. Pagans are strong here: their spiritual experiences are often revelatory and moving, even terrifying and ecstatic, and seekers are drawn to Paganism in search of such powerful experiences. Scientific rationalists might argue, as they do against other religious traditions, that Paganism falls short on "reasonableness": what we have discovered about the world using the scientific method does not generally support magickal thinking or the belief in objectively existing spiritual beings. Pagans, however, have their own pragmatic standards of reasonableness, namely that the type of devotional practices that Pagans use have provided inspiration to human beings for thousands of years. Since Pagan practices produce the luminous, joyful, and deeply meaningful experiences that so many human beings crave, their effectiveness makes them reasonable regardless of whether the associated beliefs are entirely logical. The "moral helpfulness" of Pagan religious experiences is more mixed. On the one hand, Pagans have relied upon their religious experiences to challenge mainstream moral values that they believe are wrong—the notion that the Earth is ours to exploit, for example, or the idea that human sexuality is inherently degraded and dirty. This affirmation of religious individualism is often what Pagans find most helpful, as Paganism can support a practitioner in leading a non-mainstream, but happier and more satisfying life. On the other hand, Pagans' high tolerance of moral differences can be problematic: for example, when an individual whose beliefs seemed unusual but harmless slowly becomes toxic to a group. Although Pagans do have coherent systems of ethical values, as we will explore in more detail later, the Pagan movement is both young and diffuse, and it does not have enough competent elders that new Pagans can look to as ethical role models.

In general, those who are respected as elders in the Pagan movement are those whose practices support effective leadership, harmonious community, and a stable (if sometimes nonstandard) personal life. Many Pagans are aware that developing spiritually is difficult; a period of upheaval in a person's life may be a necessary part of becoming healthy and is not necessarily evidence that an individual's beliefs are destructive. As in other religious traditions, Pagans also struggle with the influence of charismatic but flawed leaders, who may appear trustworthy until the bitter fruits of their attitudes appear. But those whose lives are consistently chaotic, or who are chronically in conflict with others, eventually suffer a loss of credibility or simply destroy the groups of which they are a part. In due course, all Pagan beliefs and practices are tested by whether they *work*—whether they help practitioners lead meaningful, satisfying lives. Like other countercultural groups, Pagans need education about how to embrace diversity without tolerating subtly destructive behavior. Groups and traditions do not survive in the long term, however, unless they produce stable and effective practitioners.

Occult Knowledge and Gnosis

In popular culture, the term *occultism* has become so associated with Satanic panics and fears of abusive, brainwashing cults that I almost hesitate to use it here. But the notion of the occult is important to many kinds of Paganism. The term literally means "hidden" or "secret," and it usually refers to knowledge of hidden things, often requiring an initiation of some kind. In religious studies, we use the more neutral term *esotericism* for these beliefs and practices, with the prefix *eso-* meaning "inward" or "inner." Most world religions have esoteric or occult traditions, focusing on knowledge that cannot be gained through the intellect alone. In the West, these include Jewish kabbalah, Christian mysticism, and Muslim Sufism.

Wiccan theologian Constance Wise has expanded the definition of occult knowledge for contemporary Paganism, which is more egalitarian and focused on the physical than traditional Western esotericism. She suggests that occult knowledge is the creative, non-rational, subliminal knowledge that arises from the experience of the human body.[1] Though Wise focuses on female bodies specifically, her concept is relevant to people of all sexes and genders. For Wise, occult knowledge is subliminal or hidden in that it cannot be directly taught, but must be gained through direct experience. David Abram's descriptions of encountering animals, plants, and natural phenomenon as conscious and actively communicating with him is one example of gaining "occult" knowledge under Wise's definition.[2] Occult knowledge cannot be gained through university studies, reading the news, or even regular attendance at a place of worship. Ritual practices give Pagans opportunities to encounter this beyond-ordinary knowledge, and when they are successful, practitioners' worldviews sometimes shift dramatically as their lives are viewed through a new lens.

These experiences of ineffable *mystery* can make practitioners feel oddly set apart from those who have not shared their shift in perspective. ("Occult knowledge" is what a practitioner comes away with after having encountered "mystery"; "mystery" is the divine reality that cannot be fully captured by the human mind.) It is possible to take this sensation in an elitist direction; practitioners who have such experiences sometimes see themselves as wiser or more spiritual than others. But spiritual development is not a contest or race, nor a series of boxes to be checked. Although the hard work of spiritual practice helps to create opportunities for such experiences, they are not achieved through work, but are gifts received by grace. Some come with revelations that subtly or dramatically change one's life (for example, the bone-deep certainty that one's body and sexuality are sacred, despite the teachings of a childhood religion). Or they may prepare us to face the realities of the human condition, such as the inevitability of our deaths and those of our loved ones. Still other experiences of mystery may simply bring a lingering sense of joy and peace.

Some Pagan traditions use the practice of *initiation* to trigger experiences of mystery and to transmit occult knowledge. (Initiation can also have other functions, such as adopting the candidate into a group.[3]) Initiations can involve ritual dramas, introductions to spirits or gods, physical or psychological ordeals, instruction in practices or mythology, and more. Occasionally initiations fail; the candidate for initiation remains unmoved, feeling awkward or silly, hoping for a spiritual experience but remaining uncomfortably in the realm of the ordinary. Although a poor ritual performance can sometimes account for an initiatory failure, at times the reasons are more subtle, having to do with the quality of the group's relationships or their spiritual preparation.

In the second half of the twentieth century, many initiatory rituals and other material that had previously been secret or *oathbound* within particular Pagan and esoteric traditions were published. The release of this material is part of what has enabled the rapid growth of the Pagan movement.

Some Pagans have spoken out for the importance of keeping initiatory material private, however. Druid John Michael Greer believes that there are psychological and spiritual benefits when a candidate does not know what is going to occur during an initiation, as well as in the practice of silence afterward.[4] The element of surprise increases the impact of a ritual in the same way that avoiding "spoilers" increases the impact of a film. Once the ritual has occurred, keeping silent about information received or experiences had tends to focus one's attention on them, leading them to become deeply integrated into one's system of beliefs and values. Finally, when a candidate is left to wrestle with a symbol or a piece of liturgy on her own or in the context of a small group, rather than immediately discussing it on the internet or getting a cut-and-dried explanation from a teacher, she has an opportunity for contemplation and slow discovery that is unusual in our busy culture. The practices of initiation and keeping knowledge oathbound create spiritual and psychological containers for transformative spiritual experiences. While it is possible to abuse the practice of secrecy—for example, to gain power over or take advantage of others—most Pagans know that a relationship in which initiation might occur needs to develop slowly so that trust can form. Some leaders have even developed criteria for evaluating whether Pagan and other religious groups are safe, such as the Advanced Bonewits Cult Danger Evaluation Frame by the late Druid Isaac Bonewits.[5]

Intuitions and information received from extraordinary sources are often called *gnosis* in Paganism, after the Greek word for "knowledge." Some Pagans differentiate Unverified (or Unverifiable) Personal Gnosis (UPG)—information received by a single person—from Peer-Corroborated Gnosis (PCG), or information that is independently received by a group of individuals.[6] Pagans often seek UPG through divination or meditation. Talk of gnosis is most common among hard polytheists, who seek out such intuitions to serve their gods, adjust ancient practices to a different time and place, and fill in gaps in broken traditions. Examples of UPG might include intuitions about ritual ("The herbs traditionally used in this ritual don't grow here, but my gnosis says that rosemary will be an acceptable substitute") or personal direction ("Brighid is calling me to learn more about my ancestors—I think my family may be connected to Ireland"). More intense forms of gnosis have much in common with powerful artistic inspiration and may include receiving complex liturgies, instructions for spiritual healing practices, narratives about the gods, or requests for acts of service. Like religious people of other traditions, some Pagans see themselves as the hands of the gods in the world and may do volunteer work, create art, cultivate land, or engage in other activities as acts of devotion.

UPG is most controversial in Pagan traditions that are reconstructionist, in other words, traditions that are attempting to reconstruct ancient religions as accurately as possible. Some reconstructionists reject gnosis as innovation that will dilute their practice or render it inauthentic. Others fear that UPG will lead to changes in practice in already small, scattered communities, making it even more difficult for groups to gather for group ritual. Still other reconstructionists are nontheists, seeing gnosis as self-delusion and wishful thinking that threatens to corrupt the religion of their ancestors. Although not all Heathens (Northern European Pagans) are strict reconstructionists, the issue of UPG has been particularly divisive in that community. Heathens have rich textual foundations for their practice in the form of the Icelandic Sagas and Eddas, formerly oral poems which were recorded during the medieval period. For some Heathens, these texts have an authority similar to the authority of the Bible for traditional Christians. Personal gnosis threatens that authority. Particularly controversial is the practice of *seiðr*, a traditional Germanic form of magickal practice that is mentioned in the sagas. Some contemporary Heathens believe they have recovered the practices of *seiðr* through peer-corroborated gnosis and have made these practices central to their Heathenry. Other Heathens reject the authenticity of reconstructed *seiðr*. In an additional twist, *seiðr* is associated with gender transgression in the traditional lore, and its practice has attracted homophobic prejudice from a minority of Heathens in the community.[7]

Pagans are engaged in ongoing discussion about how to evaluate UPG and determine its trustworthiness. For example, T. Thorn Coyle focuses on developing psychological health and spiritual self-knowledge so that intuitions can be accurately received;[8] Luisa Teish illustrates the process of testing intuition by following low-risk impulses to see where they lead;[9] and Sarah Kate Istra Winter emphasizes the importance of checking intuitions with level-headed peers or looking for support in traditional lore.[10] In this area, Pagans have much to learn from the Society of Friends (the Quakers), who have been evolving a system to confirm gnosis among peers for centuries. It is an essential part of Quaker practice to listen for the voice of the divine, and over the years, Quaker meetings have supported views that dramatically challenged the standards of American society (most famously during the Abolition movement against American slavery). Groups called "clearness committees" assist individuals in spiritual discernment, a slow, contemplative process through which Quakers collectively seek to know God's will. The presence of trusted elders, engagement with Quaker tradition and ethical principles, healthy group relationships, individual spiritual development, and an open timeline for decision-making all give structure to clearness committees.[11] Similar practices among Pagan groups could help address the destabilizing effects of too-quickly embraced gnosis.

Intimacy in Contemporary Paganism

The shift toward solitary practice in contemporary Paganism has made it more difficult for new Pagans to establish a deep, satisfying spiritual practice. Sociologist Helen Berger reports that as many as 79 percent of Pagans consider themselves to be solitaries, meaning that though they may occasionally meet with one or more groups for ritual, they do not have ongoing membership in a regularly meeting local group.[12] Pagans today most often enter the movement through books, internet resources, workshops, and distance training. This represents a dramatic change from the 1970s, when most Pagans met in small, close, explicitly countercultural groups. Since it could be dangerous to one's job and the custody of one's children to openly identify as Pagan, many of these groups were at least somewhat secretive about their existence and membership, and some also practiced secrecy around oathbound material. Some Pagan women's groups and gay and lesbian groups had a consciousness-raising and personal sharing component that also required discretion and confidentiality. Although there were no doubt times when confidentiality and silence were abused, they also had a powerful bonding effect. Small, closed groups that are bound together with confidentiality agreements often grow emotionally close and develop a family dynamic (which can help sustain the group or lead to its demise, depending on the participants' attitudes toward family). Closely bonded groups provide stabilizing containers for intense spiritual experiences, such as the initiatory process discussed earlier in this chapter.

The decline of small groups reflects many missed opportunities. Many Pagans do not have communities with whom they can celebrate rites of passage, and they often lack the real-life ties that make it possible to mobilize a group for the support of its members. Some important tools for Pagan religious practice, such as meditation, trance, energy work, and psychic sensitivity, are difficult or impossible to learn from a book. But aside from these more practical concerns, the movement away from intense in-person religious experience in a container of ongoing relationship has changed the nature of the religion. Marshall McLuhan famously said that "the medium is the message." Forms of Pagan practice that lack human intimacy do not encourage Pagan practitioners to experience intimacy with the divine; forms of practice that are not embodied lead to a Paganism that gives only lip service to the idea of the holy body.

Pagans are trying to relearn a mindset that has almost been lost from Western culture, and they are doing it largely without experienced teachers. In Chapter Two, I described how

David Abram temporarily recaptured a profound sense of intimacy with the natural world by spending time in rural parts of the United States and in Sri Lanka. During his year in Sri Lanka, he developed close relationships with shamanic practitioners, and also came to see the world as full of other-than-human persons, resulting in an intense, intimate, and embodied relationship with his environment. Upon returning to the States, however, that consciousness began to slip away in mere weeks. There is something about the analytical consciousness we absorb from our culture that alienates us from the connectedness that Abram experienced in Sri Lanka. I'm not one to say that Western culture and technology are fundamentally bad—I quite like antibiotics and the internet—but we have lost our balance, creating an intense, frantic, disconnected habitat for ourselves that deprives us of some of our humanity.

Sherry Turkle's recent book *Alone Together* examines the impact of communications technology on human psychology. Although Turkle has been pro-technology in the past, in this book she is quite critical. Her interview data shows that people, and especially young people, are living with a great deal of anxiety around their technological communications. Many feel overwhelmed by the constant barrage of communication and data, with the result that teenagers today have a strong preference for communications media that can be tightly controlled. Communications technology is experienced as invasive, leading to distancing behaviors that ironically lead the people communicating to feel less close. When we allow our technology to rule our behavior rather than setting boundaries around its use, intimate human relationships become much more difficult to form. Polytheists sometimes speak of courting their gods or the spirits of the land as if they were lovers, but how do we learn to initiate intimacy with the non-human if we have never experienced it on a human level?

Pagan Devotion

Some Pagans prefer the word "devotion" to "worship," feeling that "worship" has inappropriate connotations of subservience, while "devotion" might also be used of the feelings that one has toward a lover or a child ("I am devoted to my family"). In general, Pagan devotion aims to create intimacy between Pagans and the divine or the gods. Michael York observes that all Pagan devotional practices are also found in other world religions,[13] and that making comparisons between traditions can help us in understanding them. For example, Pagans engage in the veneration of sacred images, a practice sometimes known as *idolatry*. In popular usage, this term is negative: it describes the belief that an image or idol is itself a deity. Westerners often think of the biblical story of the golden calf, which the ancient Israelites made and worshipped as a god while Moses was away (Exodus 32).

The belief that a deity can be fully identified with an object is relatively rare, however, and usually limited to natural phenomena—for instance, the belief that a mountain deity is the soul of a particular mountain. Pagans are more likely to venerate images as some Catholics do, understanding them as foci for devotion and divine presence, but considering the deity to be much more than the physical idol. Pagan image veneration can also resemble the practice of some Hindus. At certain Hindu festivals, the image of a deity is washed, dressed, offered food, and reverently carried in a festival parade before being disposed of in the river at the day's end—the image being only a temporary vehicle for the deity, not completely identified with it. Other Hindu deity shrines are more permanent, with priests tending the same image of a deity for many years, but with the understanding that the image is not the deity's only possible place of manifestation. For Pagans, visual or tactile ways of interacting with the gods can deepen the sense of intimacy during devotions. Many Pagans prefer to pray to their gods before altars or shrines honoring them. Some also make offerings of food or drink, which may be consumed by the devotee afterward, placed outside, or burned, depending on the practitioner's tradition. Pagan prayers are often framed as conversations, and they may express love and gratitude, request an intercession in the practitioner's life, invite divine communication with the practitioner, or all three.

Pagans also cultivate their connection with the divine through art, dance, seasonal celebrations, and other creative activities, as well as through social justice, activism, and caregiving. Polytheists may see these activities as ways of serving the gods, while nontheists experience them as developing the full spiritual potential of human beings or encouraging connection to larger cycles. These acts express Pagan values and can help to solidify communities of practitioners. The notion of reciprocity underlies the acts of service; practitioners may devote themselves to their families, communities, gods, or the land to convey gratitude for blessings that have been received. Some of these reciprocal relationships become formalized into covenants, where an individual or group commit themselves to an ongoing relationship with a particular deity. Polytheist Pagans may devote themselves entirely to one deity while also acknowledging the existence of other deities (*henotheism*). It is more common, however, for Pagans to engage in what John Michael Greer calls *oligotheism*, devoting themselves to several deities while believing in many more.[14]

Some Pagan devotional practices involve seeking altered states of consciousness and developing specialized spiritual skills. These skills include oracular work, in which practitioners convey messages from deities or spirits for the benefit of others, as well as possession, in which the practitioner allows a deity or spirit to temporarily occupy his or her body. Successful possessory work can convey a powerful experience of spiritual presence and creates opportunities for deities to teach or speak to devotees more directly. These techniques require considerable training and practice, however, and can be psychologically dangerous and physically exhausting. Further, even highly experienced practitioners of these skills note that they cannot always be employed at will.[15] The belief that every

Pagan is his own priest/ess has sometimes led Pagans to believe that such skills are or should be accessible to every practitioner. In reality, those with the talent and training to perform such services well are rare.

The question of how Pagans can support the development of skilled spiritual specialists in their communities without losing the egalitarianism of Pagan culture is an ongoing problem. Some Pagans are opposed to the existence of paid Pagan clergy. Since Pagan clergy must generally work other jobs to earn a living, they are limited in their ability to seek intensive spiritual training or education in professional areas such as counseling and chaplaincy. But the concern that paid Pagan clergy will take decision-making power out of the hands of hardworking volunteers—especially those who founded and have sustained Pagan communities—is real. Today, contemporary Pagans remain split over what role professional clergy and spiritual specialists will have in the Pagan movement and in group devotional practices.

Summary

Most Pagans use personal experience as their primary source for knowledge about the gods and the divine. This knowledge is contextualized by folklore, academic research, and community traditions. Knowledge that is received from extraordinary sources is known as *gnosis.* Pagans disagree about the proper role of gnosis in their religion, with some making it the centerpiece of their belief system and others rejecting it entirely. Contemporary Paganism is still evolving mechanisms for evaluating gnosis. Religious experiences can ultimately be judged by their effects on the lives of practitioners, but in the short-term, they can be checked against existing traditions and submitted to group discernment processes. Additionally, practitioners can cultivate accuracy in their intuitions by developing greater psychological and spiritual health. Because of the decline of small groups in contemporary Paganism, however, many practitioners lack the intimate ties needed to structure and ground intense spiritual experiences. The development of a professional class of Pagan priest/esses and clergy may help to address this problem, but Pagans fear that in the process of institutionalization, the egalitarianism of their communities will be lost. Additionally, Pagans are skeptical of the need for professional clergy because they believe that people do not require mediators between themselves and the gods. Every practitioner is capable of forming relationship with the divine through devotion.

Activities

Read one or more of the accounts of Pagan religious experience listed below. (Both traditionally published autobiographies and blog posts are included.) Is the writer's experience familiar to you, or alien? What attracts, surprises, puzzles, or repels you about this piece of writing? What values does it express? How do those values differ from your own?

How do you evaluate your own spiritual experiences (or if you feel you haven't had one, how would you evaluate one if you did)? Do you have a community of support with whom to discuss such experiences? Where would you reach out to find such a community? Organize a book group to read and discuss a Pagan spiritual autobiography. Consider writing your own.

Think about ways to begin or deepen your devotional practices. Try a spiritual art technique such as Soul Collage, plant a garden, or sign up to help a charity that reflects your values. Alternatively, research devotional practices used for a deity that you honor and try out a method that is unfamiliar to you. Experiment with building an altar, writing a prayer, or pouring a libation. How could devotion become part of the everyday fabric of your life?

Further Reading

Devotion, Prayer, and UPG

Harrow, Judy. *Devoted to You: Honoring Deity in Wiccan Practice.* New York: Citadel Press, 2003.

Krasskova, Galina. *Sigdrifa's Prayer: An Exploration & Exegesis.* Second Edition. Hubbardston, MA: Asphodel Press, 2007.

Pole, Larisa (Mist). "Cultural Appropriation in the Neopagan Community: An Asatrú Perspective." *Talking about the Elephant: An Anthology of Neopagan Perspectives on Cultural Appropriation.* Ed. Lupa. Stafford, UK: Immanion Press, 2008. 58-76.

Devotionals from Biblioteca Alexandrina (http://neosalexandria.wordpress.com/bibliotheca-alexandrina/current-titles/) and Asphodel Press (http://www.asphodel press.com/devotionals.html)

Pagan Spiritual Autobiography

Curott, Phyllis. *Book of Shadows: A Modern Woman's Journey into the Wisdom of Witchcraft and the Magic of the Goddess.* New York: Broadway Books, 2001.

DiZerega, Gus. "Encountering Pagan Deities." *Pointedly Pagan (Patheos.com).* 23 Aug 2012. http://www.patheos.com/Pagan/Encountering-Pagan-Deities-Gus-diZerega-08-24-2012.html.

Dw3t-Hthr. "Meant for Someone Else." *Letters from Gehanna.* 2 Jul 2008. http://lettersfromgehenna.blogspot.com/2008/07/meant-for-someone-else.html.

Helasdottir, Lydia. "Becoming a Horse." Excerpt from Raven Kaldera, *Wightridden: Paths of Northern-Tradition Shamanism.* Hubbardston, MA: Asphodel Press, 2007. Available at http://www.northernshamanism.org/shamanic-techniques/spirit-possession/becoming-a-horse.html.

Mee, Alison. "Journey, Story." *EarthSpirit Voices.* 15 Nov 2011. Available at http://earthspiritcommunity.blogspot.com/2011/11/journey-story.html.

Orr, Emma Restall. *Druid Priestess.* London: Thorsons, 2001.

Pitch Black Witch. "How I Got to Be a Neopagan Witch." Six-post Series. 12-18 Oct 2008. http://pitch313.blogspot.com/2008/10/how-i-go-o-be-neo-pagan-witch-part-1.html.

Chapter Four

Life, Death, and the Human Body

The human body is a sacred site for contemporary Pagans.

In contemporary Paganism, the question of "What does it mean to be human?" is intimately connected with the human body. All our experiences are filtered through the living flesh with which we experience the world; even extraordinary experiences of the non-physical are processed by the wet grey masses of our brains and interpreted using the framework of our five senses. When Pagans affirm that divinity is immanent in all things, the human body is no exception.

For some Pagan traditions, the body is human beings' most sacred place of worship and devotion. Many Pagans believe that in our physicality, and especially our sexuality, we participate in the primal forces that create the universe. Although this theology is not universal among Pagans, the affirmation that the body is holy and that pleasure is a human birthright is widespread in contemporary Paganism. Accordingly, Pagans have been more progressive than many other religious groups in supporting same-sex and consensual multiple-partner relationships, welcoming sexual minorities and transgender people as clergy, and considering whether unusual erotic practices such as sexual ritual and BDSM practice can be legitimate tools for spiritual experience. Further, because many Pagans believe that all bodies are sacred, Pagan communities tend to be more affirming of different body types than mainstream Western culture. Some Pagan communities provide safe spaces for people of all body types to go "skyclad," or nude, in a sacred setting.

Pagan attitudes about the holiness of the body also inform practices around birth and death. In some Western religions, the body is seen as a mere vessel for the soul, which is the true source of personhood. At times, the body is even believed to be degraded and inferior to the soul, which can help to justify the body's neglect or abuse. For many Pagans, however, the body is the source of human personhood (or one of the most important sources). A healthy body is thought to have a tendency toward balance and vitality that can be encouraged with holistic care. Out of a belief that normal body processes should not be treated as if they were illnesses, many Pagan women choose natural or minimally medicalized childbirth. Some Pagans seek training as nurse-midwives or doulas (birth assistants), who offer clients the opportunity to experience birth in an explicitly sacred context. Pagans also tend to prefer fewer extreme medical interventions than other Westerners when preparing for death. They are likely to sign living wills stipulating that no extraordinary means be used to keep them alive, and during terminal illnesses, they often prefer hospice care at home to dying in a hospital. Although it is a difficult task to be present for a dying person and his or her family, many Pagans consider the role of "midwifing" another's death to be a special honor. Death and birth are seen as similarly difficult transitions that the human body must undergo. Though there is no standard way in which contemporary Pagans treat the bodies of deceased loved ones, they often favor environmentally friendly techniques such as flameless cremation or green burial.

Because Pagans strongly value human relationships, many Pagans will sustain those relationships after death by ritually honoring deceased family members and friends. New Pagans sometimes resist the idea of honoring their blood ancestors because of strained family relationships or because their ancestors practiced a different religion. Pagans who advocate ancestor devotion, however, emphasize that regardless of whether we like our ancestors, without them, we ourselves would not be. Our bodies were born from theirs; we share their DNA and even, at times, their faces. Adopted family members are honored equally in Pagan ancestor devotion, as an acknowledgement that loving relationships are no less significant than blood ties. Pagans also sometimes honor their "ancestors of spirit," who may be teachers of Pagan traditions or other role models they admire, or their "ancestors of place," those who used to live on the land where Pagans now live. Combined with Pagan practices around birth, death, and sexuality, Pagan ancestor veneration expresses the belief that it is holy to be human.

Erotic Theology and its Origins

When British Wicca was first made public by Gerald Gardner in England in the 1950s, it triggered the beginning of a Pagan revival that continues to grow and diversify to this day. Because Wicca was the first contemporary Pagan religion that many people heard of, the word "Wicca" became somewhat detached from the original tradition with its specific practices and beliefs. Today, many people use "Wicca" to refer to any kind of religious witchcraft, and at times they even use the word as a synonym for "Paganism." Most Pagans consider this latter usage to be incorrect, but because the confusion has become so common, Wiccans following the traditions of Gardner's covens often use the label "British Traditional Wicca" to distinguish themselves. Some Pagans see British Traditional Wicca as lacking in historical grounding, however. Particularly among reconstructionist Pagans, the dominance of Wiccan-influenced ways of thinking in Paganism is considered an obstacle to historically authentic practice. British Wicca has nevertheless left a lasting mark on contemporary Paganism, and its theology flavors the beliefs and practices of many Pagans who do not identify as Wiccan.

"The Charge of the Goddess" is contemporary Paganism's most widely known piece of liturgy. Adapted from several older texts by Wiccan High Priestess Doreen Valiente in the 1950s, the Charge is beautifully written, and its continuing influence has much to do with Valiente's deft poetic ear. Even more important, however, are the Charge's positive images of sexuality and affirmations of female power. The text is written in the voice of the Goddess. In rituals, it is usually recited aloud by a priest/ess, who delivers the speech as the Goddess's instructions to the coven. Many Pagans today take the Charge as an ethical proof text that affirms all loving, consensual sexual acts. As the Charge reads,

> And ye shall be free from slavery; and as a sign that ye be really free, ye shall be naked in your rites; and ye shall dance, sing, feast, make music and love, all in my praise.
>
> For mine is the ecstasy of the spirit, and mine also is joy on earth; for my Law is Love unto all Beings. [...] Let my worship be within the heart that rejoiceth; for behold, all acts of love and pleasure are my rituals.[1]

In Wicca, lovemaking and celebration can be devotional acts (though this does not include indulging to excess in ways that are destructive to the body or to relationships). Sexual ritual also plays an important part in the tradition. In the Wiccan ritual of the Great Rite, celebrants carry out one of two symbolic acts: they perform a ceremony where a blade is inserted into a cup, or they engage in ritual sexual intercourse (usually in private). The Great Rite allows Wiccans to participate in the erotic union of the God and the Goddess, seen as primal powers whose interactions underlie the ongoing creation of the universe.

Other religious traditions, both Pagan and otherwise, also embrace the idea that the universe is created and sustained by erotic forces. Pagan theologian Starhawk works with the idea of a connective web of life force that she calls *the erotic,* which is something both deeper and broader than sexuality.[2] In her theology, the erotic is the movement of energy between and among many beings, not just the primal pair envisioned in Wicca. Feminist poet Audre Lorde also speaks of "the erotic as power"—as an impulse to flourish, a lust for joy and pleasure, and a resilience that strengthens human beings to resist injustice and oppression.[3] The term has also been taken up within queer

Christian theology, where it is used to describe God/dess's love for all creation and the divine desire to incarnate into flesh.[4]

In all these cases, *eros* describes a state of intimate, embodied relationship that puts the participants in touch with the flow of divine life force. Although sexuality is one place where Pagans experience the erotic, it is present in any moment of deep intimacy, and not just with other human beings. The erotic is present when holding a friend's hand and looking into her eyes, but it is also present when we connect with our environments in full awareness. The delicate touch of a honeybee as it lands on my arm, seeking sustenance; the mischievous play of the wind in my hair; the cushion of warm earth and fresh grass under my body as I stretch out in the sun— all these are opportunities to approach ocean, land, and sky as I would a human beloved. Eros is the mechanism through which many Pagans experience the divine in the world.

In Pagan traditions that embrace erotic theology, it is common to seek religious experiences through sexual activities. Many Pagans enjoy engaging in sex with their partners in a ritual context. Further, while some Pagans use BDSM techniques such as bondage or spanking purely for pleasure, others employ them to achieve altered states of consciousness. This kind of alternative erotic behavior remains controversial in contemporary Paganism, although it is much more accepted among Pagans than within mainstream culture. Those who advocate for BDSM as a healthy form of sexual expression are often part of BDSM-focused communities that hold individuals accountable for their ethics. "Safe, sane, and consensual" is a common motto. Within these communities, erotic activities are carefully negotiated in a context that emphasizes good communication, informed consent, and individual autonomy.[5]

Pagans are also relatively accepting of other sexual minorities, such as those in same-sex or ethically nonmonogamous relationships (often known as "polyamory"). Since many Pagans see pleasure as a divine gift, any sexual practice that does not hurt the individuals involved or the community is usually judged acceptable. Some Pagan groups, however, do not grant sexuality any special religious status, and they are more likely to see alternative sexual practices as disruptive to community. For example, although the Heathen community includes queer and BDSM-affirming practitioners, it tends to attract Pagans who prefer conventional gender roles and more mainstream standards of sexual behavior. In such traditions, non-sexual physical techniques such as fasting, tests of endurance, or other ordeals may still be used to help induce religious experiences.

Gender

Contemporary American Paganism as we know it was born in the California counterculture of the 1960s and 1970s. Many people were drawn to Paganism because it offered different views of sexuality and gender than mainstream religions. Ever since, gender politics have been a powerful force in the movement. Initially, many women and men embraced Paganism and Goddess worship as paths that included images of feminine divinity, which were weak or absent in the religions of their birth. As theologian Carol Christ argued, women needed the Goddess in order to take pride in their bodies and be confident in their own power. Women worshipped goddesses to empower themselves to fight for gender equality, as well as for personal liberation. Additionally, contemporary Paganism offered men unconventional images of masculinity, emphasizing fertility and virility rather than violence and domination. For a generation or more of practitioners, contemporary Paganism was a religion that challenged traditional ideas about gender and offered refreshing, potent alternatives.

As gay, lesbian, bisexual, transgender, and queer-identified practitioners joined the movement, Pagan ideas about gender became more complex. Beliefs that had once seemed revolutionary began to feel constrictive. Women-only Dianic rituals that celebrated "women's mysteries"—experiences that focus on cycles of menstruation and childbirth—came under criticism for gender essentialism. *Gender essentialism* is the belief that gender is wholly biological; differences in biology are thought to give men and women strongly differing experiences of the world. A younger generation of Pagans rejected these beliefs around gender. These *gender constructivist* Pagans argued that gender is mostly a matter of social role, and that men and women are equally capable of having "feminine" and "masculine" qualities (especially if supported by their communities in doing so). Believing that masculinity and femininity were principles found in every human being, progressive Wiccans challenged the idea that the Great Rite required a male priest and a female priestess. Covens that welcomed this shift made it possible for lesbian or gay couples to lead their groups for the first time. Witchcraft traditions also began to experience backlash from some men who felt that the available masculine roles were not strong enough. Today, a wider variety of contemporary Pagan traditions have developed, and men can now approach various reconstructionist groups for practices based on a warrior ethic.

Most recently, controversies around gender in Paganism have focused on gender-based exclusion from public events. At the California Pagan conference PantheaCon, tension had been slowly rising around the issue of single-gender rituals. Women devoted to male gods had occasionally been turned away from devotional rituals to those gods because they themselves were not male, as had men from rituals for goddesses. The tension came to a head in 2011, however, around the exclusion of transgender women from Dianic women-only rituals. Some participants felt that transwomen should be permitted in women-only rituals because they have feminine energy or feminine souls. Those who opposed transgender inclusion in the rituals argued variously that transwomen do not menstruate and cannot participate in women's blood mysteries, which are based around physical fertility; or that transwomen were not raised as girls and cannot relate to the experience of growing up and experiencing puberty in a female body. Some women who argued against transgender inclusion also stated that because of past traumas, they could never feel safe in ritual space with any person who had ever been male. A few claimed that transwomen were attempting to use "male" privilege to invade and destroy women's space.

Transgender activists responded that although transwomen's histories of oppression and persecution are different from women who were born with female bodies, they are certainly not a "privileged" group; in fact, transgender people who are recognized as transgender are attacked and murdered with disturbing frequency, and they often experience employment discrimination and harassment in social situations. Additionally, those supporting transgender inclusion emphasized that there is no one universal experience of "womanhood." Not all women want or will have children; not all women born with female bodies menstruate, or have ever menstruated; not all women have been made to feel ashamed of their bodies or have survived sexual assault. Race, class, culture, sexual orientation, and biological realities all change women's sense of what it means to be a woman. According to those in favor of transgender inclusion, transwomen have an equally valid claim to womanhood.[6]

Since 2011, active dialogue about gender in Paganism has been ongoing. After PantheaCon 2012, the PantheaCon organizers passed a new gender discrimination policy, specifying that public women-only and men-only events at Pantheacon will be open to all those who identify as such. (Private events held during the conference are not subject to the policy.)[7] Women who wish to retain restricted space for those born with female bodies have had heartfelt talks with transwomen, sometimes with positive results.[8] As dialogue continues, the language around gender-exclusive rituals has begun to shift. Rather than "women's mysteries," Dianics have begun to speak instead of "womb mysteries," thus separating the experience of a concrete biological process from the more fluid experience of gender. The attempt to decouple "womanhood" from having a functional uterus and "manhood" from having a functional penis has helped to diffuse tension around the issue, as have efforts to hold explicitly gender-inclusive rituals for the public. Transgender and queer Pagans are also developing rituals celebrating specifically transgender and queer experience. Resources for these rituals include Raven Kaldera's *Hermaphrodeities* and P. Sufenas Virius Lupus's *All-Soul, All-Body, All-Love, All-Power: A TransMythology.* The issue of how to define new gender roles in Paganism is still unresolved, however, and will likely remain a topic of controversy and debate among Pagans for years to come.[9]

The Multiple Soul

Pagans have a range of beliefs about the human soul that parallels their beliefs about divinity. Some Pagans see the soul and the body as being completely identified—the soul is the body and the body is the soul, in the same way that pantheists believe that God/dess is the world and the world is God/dess. Others share the common Western belief that the soul is influenced by the body, but is more than the body, and will continue on in altered form after the body's death (similar to panentheists' belief that God/dess is in the world, and the world is in God/dess, but God/dess is more than the world). A third view is that personhood exists only in the body, and that there is no spiritual substance we can meaningfully call a "soul" (similar to the nontheist position).

The theology of multiple souls is gaining prevalence in the Pagan community, however. In this model, human beings have multiple spiritual essences that serve different functions. This notion is found in a number of religious traditions. Scholar Claude Lecouteux describes its appearance in ancient and medieval Northern European religion, where people were thought to have three spirits. The *fylgja* was an individual's double that also served as a protective guardian spirit; the *hugr* was the active force of the individual that carried his or her personality out into the world; and the *hamr* was an inner spiritual form that determined a person's outward appearance, but was also capable of traveling outside the body.[10] In ancient Egyptian religion, a person was thought to have three souls (the *ka*, the *ba*, and the *akh*), as well as other spiritual components such as the heart and the name, each of which had different functions in life and in the afterlife.[11] In the charming book *The Traveller's Guide to the Duat,* Kemetic reconstructionist Kiya Nicoll details the preparation the parts of the human being must undergo for being separated at death, transformed, and reintegrated in the land of the dead. The body is carefully preserved and left behind in the living world, where its persistence supports the stable and happy existence of the deceased's transformed and reassembled self.

A somewhat less complex multiple soul model can also be found in the Western ceremonial magick practiced by some contemporary Pagans. Many forms of ceremonial magick borrow from Jewish mysticism, where the three parts of the soul are known as *nefesh, ruach,* and *neshamah.* Simply put, the nefesh is the animal self, the ruach is the human self, and the neshamah is the divine self that survives death. Craft teachers Victor and Cora Anderson derived a similar three-soul model from Hawaiian Huna, in which the animal self is *Unihipili,* the human self *Uhane,* and the divine self *Aumakua.* Their writings on the subject were published in a volume entitled *Etheric Anatomy,* and were also spread by Starhawk in *The Spiral Dance,* where she names the selves Younger Self, Talking Self, and Deep Self. In the Andersons' model, the body is thought to be of the same substance as the selves, only made of denser matter. Fostering communication and cooperation between the selves (including the body) is necessary for spiritual health, as well as for the effective practice of magick.

In multiple-soul models, the souls have different fates after death. Pagans who also believe in reincarnation tend to identify the "divine" self as the part that reincarnates, not the "human" self (which holds the personality of a single lifetime) or the "animal" self, both of which may return to the earth after the death of the body. In some traditions, it is believed a traumatic death may cause the separation of the souls from the body to go awry, and the animal or human selves may remain stranded on the material plane as ghosts. These stranded souls are merely echoes of a person, however, as the divine part of the self has already moved on. This belief is similar to one in Chinese religion, where the *p'o* soul can become angered and transform into a demon if not properly treated after the body's death.[12] Some Pagans also embrace the spiritualist belief that after death, one or more parts of the soul travel in the spiritual realms for a time before incarnating into a new human body. Reincarnation beliefs influenced by Spiritualism, Buddhism, and Hinduism are common in the Pagan community, and they are often combined with images of the underworld or afterlife realms from ancient religions. For many contemporary Pagans, these realms are temporary resting places where the soul or souls review the life just lived and choose whether to return to earth.[13]

Ancestor Veneration

Beliefs about the ancestors vary among traditions and individuals. Some Pagans honor their ancestors as a way of affirming their ethnic and religious heritage. Although they may not believe that their ancestors continue to objectively exist after death, they honor them in their communities as a way of keeping their memory and their contributions alive. Other Pagans believe that they can continue to communicate with their ancestors on a spiritual level. Pagans who affirm a multiple-soul model may believe that the human souls of their ancestors remain contactable in order to offer advice and assistance to living loved ones, but their divine souls reincarnate. Others think that their ancestors do not reincarnate at all, but continue to learn and grow in the spiritual realms while maintaining contact with the living world.

Many Pagans honor their ancestors around Samhain, the Celtic festival from which secular Halloween is derived. Rituals may include reading the names of loved ones who passed during the past year; telling stories about deceased loved ones; or building altars of flowers, photographs, and food in the style of Mexican *Día de los Muertos* shrines. Some Pagans hold "dumb suppers," in which participants cook their ancestors' favorite foods and then eat together in silence, with a full plate set out and a chair left empty for their beloved dead. Ancestor veneration is not a purely seasonal practice, however. Some Pagans build year-round altars for their dead, which may be as simple as a row of photographs along a mantelpiece. As when honoring deities, practitioners may leave offerings of fresh water or favorite food or drinks for their ancestors. These offerings may later be eaten, or may be placed outside or buried. Pagans who engage in these practices often feel that they are helping their ancestors remain connected to the living community, and that they are able to invite their ancestors' help and protection in their lives. Ancestor worker Laura Patsouris further asserts that knowing one's dead is essential to knowing and loving oneself. She writes, "Without embracing your ancestors, self knowledge and self-love are difficult: how can you truly know yourself with no context? [...]Each one of us is a miracle, a story of survival retold over countless generations; the product of perseverance, luck, toil and love."[14] For many Pagans, honoring one's ancestors is yet another way to both grapple with the challenges of the human condition and to celebrate its joys.

Summary

Pagans largely consider the human body to be holy, and many engage in physical techniques to alter consciousness or show devotion to their gods. Respect for the body's natural wisdom also guides Pagan choices around childbirth and end of life care.

Some Pagans see human sexuality as a way to participate in the universe's ongoing processes of creation. They may see the erotic (embodied, intimate sensuality) as an expression of the life force that permeates all of being. Pagans who believe that lovingly shared pleasure is a human birthright tend to welcome sexual minorities as clergy, as well as affirming all consensual sexual practices. Other Pagans prefer mainstream standards of sexual behavior, but their religion may still have a pronounced physical component in the form of ritual ordeals or acts of physical endurance.

Gender politics are a source of controversy in Paganism, with ongoing debates over whether gender is primarily biological, primarily social, or a balance of each. Although nearly all forms of Paganism offer challenges to traditional gender roles, Pagans have begun to find once-revolutionary rewritings of masculinity and femininity to be constrictive. Currently, how to include transgender persons in single-gender rituals and the exploration of specifically transgender and queer religious mysteries are important concerns.

Pagans use a variety of models to understand the makeup of human beings on a spiritual level, but many of the better-developed theologies involve multiple souls, which have different functions in life and different fates after death. Reincarnation is the most common Pagan afterlife belief, though not all Pagans believe that reincarnation happens right away, or that it is mandatory. Many Pagans also engage in ancestor veneration, which maintains a relationship between the living and the dead and helps to nurture continuity in religious and cultural traditions.

Activities

How do you honor your body? So often our culture frames "taking care of ourselves" in terms of deprivation and struggle—crash diets, "no pain no gain" workouts, and unpleasant or even painful cosmetic techniques. Consider ways to instead give your body gifts: expand your grocery budget and visit a farmer's market for meat, produce, honey, and cheeses that are both healthy and delicious; experiment with sports, dance, yoga, and more until you find a physical activity you genuinely love; or buy stylish clothes that fit you well, even if you're not the size and shape you wish you were.

As we learn about our bodies, we also learn about our ancestors. Genealogy services now offer DNA testing and analysis that can tell us a great deal about our health and the ethnic groups that we came from, as well as help to find living relatives. Ask your relatives for family stories, or learn to make a traditional family dish. If you are estranged from your family, consider engaging in ancestor work to reconnect with your origins, even if you cannot connect with living family at this time. Take steps to support your own immediate family after you are gone: make a will, a living will, and/or a document outlining your wishes in the event of your death. Share your wishes with your loved ones, and use the opportunity to learn about their attitudes around death and dying.

For Further Reading

Hunter, Jennifer. *Rites of Pleasure: Sexuality in Wicca and NeoPaganism.* New York: Citadel Press, 2004.

Patsouris, Laura. *Weaving Memory: A Guide to Honoring the Ancestors.* Hubbardston, MA: Asphodel Press, 2010.

Starhawk, M. Macha NightMare, and the Reclaiming Collective. *The Pagan Book of Living and Dying.* San Francisco: HarperSanFrancisco, 1997.

Thompson, Sarah et al (eds). *Gender and Transgender in Modern Paganism.* Cupertino, CA: Circle of Cerridwen Press, 2012. Available at http://st4r.org/genderbook.pdf.

Whedon, Sarah. *Birth on the Labyrinth Path: Sacred Embodiment in the Childbearing Year.* Patheos Press, 2012.

Chapter Five

Ethics and Justice

Virtues and values create a flexible basis for Pagan ethical decisions.

Contemporary Pagan ethics are based in virtue ethics. Virtue ethics emphasize the moral character of a person. This approach is different from rule-based ethical systems ("Thou shalt"/"Thou shalt not"), as well as from systems that are primarily concerned with consequences, where behavior is recommended or forbidden based on its expected effect. Instead, virtue ethics focus on cultivating positive human characteristics. A person's virtues pervade her life and worldview. For example, a loving person does not perform loving acts because someone has commanded it, nor because she will receive favors, gifts, or social status in return. Love as a virtue is not a superficial quality. When cultivated, it results in a consistent outlook and behavior from the person who manifests it. In the West, virtue ethics originate with Plato and Aristotle, though this approach to ethics can also be found in ancient Chinese thought.

Discovering the Will

One common ethical principle among Wiccans and eclectic Pagans comes from British Traditional Wicca. The Wiccan Rede is most commonly phrased as "An it harm none, do what you will," where "an" means "if."[1] Other traditions prefer the contemporary language of "Harm none and do what you will" to emphasize that both harming none and doing one's will are active goals. Although this principle can be shallowly interpreted to mean, "Do whatever you want as long as it doesn't hurt anyone," a more nuanced interpretation explains the word "will" as a state of alignment and contact with the divine. A person's Will (sometimes capitalized to differentiate it from mere whim) is not based on the impulse of the moment, but rather on deep and enduring desires to love and be loved, to create beautiful or useful things, or to make change in the world. When Pagan traditions talk about will, they are speaking of the unfolding purpose of a human life in conversation with the divine. Discovery of one's true will is the project of the lifetime, and it involves developing the personal strengths that philosophers have called virtues.

For those influenced by Western ceremonial magick, the discernment of an individual's true will is part of the Great Work of the universe. Similar to Pagan erotic theology, where Pagans' erotic expression allows them to participate in divine creation, discovering their true will allows practitioners to participate in the self-discovery of the universe. Some Pagans embrace Aleister Crowley's Law of Thelema, which reads, "Do what thou wilt shall be the whole of the Law. Love is the Law, Love under Will."[2] This statement is often taken to mean that if an individual successfully discovers her true will, she will take on the essentially loving nature of Being. Other Pagans, however, believe that human discernment is never perfect; it is inevitable that we come into conflict with well-intentioned others while attempting to do the work we are called to do. Accordingly, Wiccans are instructed to "harm none" while doing their will, as a warning that the freedom to swing one's fist ends at the other person's nose. In this paradigm, our personal freedoms are limited by the need to ensure freedom for others.

Neglected Virtues

Brendan Myers's *The Other Side of Virtue* attempts to recontextualize some of the virtues that were valued by pre-Christian societies for contemporary Pagans. His work draws on Greek, Celtic, and Northern European cultures to recover traditional systems of ethics and their virtues. For example, in heroic literature, honor is defined as an inherently social quality. An honorable person is one who exhibits loyalty, honesty, reliability, and trustworthiness in his relationships with others. In Northern European traditions, the word for honor is "troth," which is related to the English word "truth." To be honorable suggests that one demonstrates integrity in all of one's dealings. According to Myers, however, honor is something that is given to an honorable person, not a virtue that can be cultivated in a vacuum. It is tied up with reputation and with community respect.[3] In our highly individualistic Western culture, this virtue is rarely recognized, let alone cultivated. Busy, harried schedules lead many of us to routinely break commitments to friends, and the dependable structures of relationship that are necessary for sustainable community are slow to form. Our relative isolation from each other and narrow focus on our individual households means we have few opportunities to gain honor—and yet this virtue is central to many of the myths that contemporary Pagans value. How to cultivate such virtues within a wider culture that does not support them is one of the ongoing struggles of contemporary Paganism.

The contrast between Pagan values and mainstream Western values is particularly noticeable around issues of sexuality and the body. A person who is passionately physical and delights in loving sexuality can be seen as expressing important human qualities. Yet the words that were once used to positively describe this virtue—such as "lusty"—have a negative connotation in modern English. At times, neglected virtues can be reclaimed. The older meaning of "pride," for example, has recently been revived by pride movements such as Gay Pride and Pagan Pride. In Western culture, "pride" is often synonymous with "hubris," the arrogance that precedes a disastrous fall. But pride is more properly understood as the state of owning one's self and identity without apology or shame. Although community is not as essential for the cultivation of pride as it is for honor, gathering with like-minded others makes taking pride in oneself a far easier task—and sustainable pride requires choosing friends who treat each other with respect.

Contemporary Pagan ethics are inherently pluralistic. Not all virtues can be expressed at the same time, and different virtues may even suggest different courses of action. Many Pagans are polytheists, and their gods express diverse strengths and virtues. The cultivation of these virtues can support multiple ways of being ethical. For example, a practitioner might cultivate creativity and fierce compassion in honor of Brighid, poet and healer, or clear thinking and communication in honor of Hermes, patron of orators and inventors. In some cases, Pagans seek to hold paradox by cultivating the capacity for virtues that superficially contradict. In Wicca's "Charge of the Goddess," the Goddess calls witches to have "beauty and strength, power and compassion, honor and humility, mirth and reverence within you."[4] According to the Charge, a virtuous person must be capable of a variety of qualities depending on context. A successful group leader, for example, sees his leadership as service to the group; he puts his own agenda partially aside in order to create a harmonious atmosphere and empower individuals to work together effectively. Good leadership requires humility. However, a good group leader also has a backbone, and he is willing to use the respect the group gives him to protect it when he must. A group member who becomes disruptive or even abusive must be held accountable for that behavior by the leader, who is supported by the group as a whole. A good leader must accept that power and be willing to use the authority he has been granted. Finding the balance between virtues—for every virtue also has a shadow side—is one of the challenges of virtue ethics. Unbalanced humility can become subservience; unbalanced power can become egotism and tyranny.

Virtue-based ethics make for a highly flexible ethical system. Based on principles rather than rules, virtue ethics can easily adjust to the particularities of situations: people, places, and times. To those who were raised in a rule-based system, where ethical decisions are often framed in black and white terms, virtue ethics can appear to lack a foundation, almost like having no ethics at all. If there are many ways of being ethical, how can a person choose between them? Even worse, isn't it possible to mistake a vice for a virtue and end up tolerating destructive behavior? Yet virtue ethics are not entirely subjective or relativistic. Ultimately, all virtues are properly cultivated in community. Healthy religious communities have elders and ancestors who embody the virtues that they value. Virtuous behavior is modeled on the actions of these role models, and the virtuous behavior of members of the community is acknowledged and praised by other members. Life experience and time-tested community traditions help young people learn virtuous behavior.

It is nevertheless possible for both individuals and communities to hold up a "virtue" that is destructive. In our own culture, for example, the ability to accumulate individual wealth is often admired as a virtue, regardless of whether that wealth is used for the good of the community. Ancient philosophers such as Aristotle differentiated false virtues from true with the concept of *eudaimonia*.[5] Sometimes this term is translated as happiness, but a more accurate translation is "flourishing." A thoroughly virtuous person can be recognized by the fact that she is flourishing on many levels. The term is an expression of spiritual, mental, and physical health, not simply of a passing emotion. (Some ancient philosophers believed that that spiritual health necessarily correlates with physical health and prosperity, but I disagree. It is certainly possible to actively choose poverty out of a spiritual calling and find that poverty freeing. A spiritually healthy poverty is part of a stable lifestyle, however; it does not involve racking up credit card bills that one cannot pay. Additionally, although poor physical health can have psychological or spiritual roots, illness is a natural part of human life. A spiritually healthy person may struggle with poor physical health, but she is able to face her health crises with compassion, grace, and humor. More than outward signs of material wealth or physical health, "flourishing" is best expressed by the joy and engaged sense of presence that a spiritually healthy person brings to her community.)

In contrast to this flourishing, the pursuit of false virtues brings only a shallow and passing happiness. According to virtue ethicists, the pursuit of material wealth or worldly power for reasons other than the health of the community does not result in flourishing, but rather a persistent sense of emptiness and a lifetime of regrets. The possession of personal virtue, however, is thought to foster alignment with the divine, peace of mind, and satisfaction regardless of whether virtuous behavior is consistently acknowledged by others or results in a clearly good outcome. When greed is held up as a virtue in community, the soul sickness and social injustice that result are signs that the community has lost its way. As we know from our own society, this sickness can be difficult to correct, particularly when those embracing the false virtue have gained positions of power and are no longer accountable to those around them. Virtue ethics function most effectively in small communities with a high degree of social accountability, as well as in the presence of experienced elders whose advice and wisdom are taken seriously. As contemporary Paganism moves through its adolescence as a religious movement, the need for fair-minded elders to stabilize scattered religious communities and help to ensure accountability grows ever greater.

Justice

The virtue of justice is one of those that can only arise from a healthy community. In Pagan belief, the divine is immanent in the world, and all things are interconnected. While it is impossible to completely avoid doing harm, entangled as we are in a world where resources are finite, Pagans cannot effectively tend their own well-being at the expense of others. In an interconnected world, to do harm to another is in some way to harm oneself. Justice, then, arises from a community that tends to the quality of relationships while simultaneously balancing the rights and freedoms of individuals.

This complex balancing act involves personal and social accountability for behavior and a commitment to the respectful and fair treatment of others. Yet it also requires individuals to have a considerable degree of self-knowledge and self-respect. A just community is difficult to maintain if individuals do not speak up for their own diverse needs, and instead expect the community to anticipate those needs and defend them. Justice also requires the shared belief that no individual or group's rights are inherently more important than all others'. In mainstream society, laws and social systems are set up to automatically privilege the rights and freedoms of some groups, while others must struggle for or are denied similar opportunities. In subcultures that are pushing back against mainstream racial, gender, and class hierarchies, however, we sometimes automatically prioritize the rights and freedoms of those who claim victim status. This strategy can help those who have been denied power, sometimes for generations, to move into a position of equality. However, it is important to use this strategy in a conscious manner. Marginalized groups can move into a position of greater equality when their rights and freedoms are particularly safeguarded, but it is important to bring both individual and communal self-awareness to this process. When claims of victimhood or emotional appeals are used to shut down difficult conversations rather than furthering dialogue, communities cannot effectively correct unjust power imbalances. Similarly, justice is out of reach when it becomes more important to individuals or groups to win a debate than it is to maintain relationships of respect.

The desire to seek justice through right relationship with the land, other human beings, and the divine has been particularly pressing for feminist Pagan theologians. These theologians are grounded by the belief that individual actions always have an effect on the whole. For Constance Wise, developing a bone-deep familiarity with interdependence is one of the most important reasons to seek occult knowledge.[6] Interdependence is not a political philosophy or a spiritual metaphor for Pagans, but rather a lived experience. The rain falling from the sky and being absorbed into the land, running into lakes and rivers from which we drink, and our sweat evaporating again into the atmosphere; the pollinating bees sustaining the plants that grow our food, then bacteria breaking down the waste we produce, to be grown again into flowers that feed the bees; our own bodies, communicating in every moment with the wind and sun, our posture, mood, and even health subtly shifting with temperature and weather: all the parts of the living world are in constant interaction, influencing each other, their actions resonating throughout a network of relationships. Our conscious minds are poorly equipped for recognizing our immersion in both human and other-than-human relationships. Yet the spiritual capacities that Pagans cultivate in ritual can give access to this alternative way of knowing. In turn, knowledge of mystery—of divine immanence and interdependence—can shape our ethical decisions and lead us toward justice.

The Problem of Evil

In Western theology, *theodicy* refers to the problem of evil, namely: how can a benevolent God allow terrible things to happen? Evil is rarely a "problem" in this sense in Paganism, because few Pagans believe in a deity who is both omniscient (all-knowing) and omnipotent (all-powerful), and who therefore should be able to stop human suffering. Nor do Pagans necessarily believe that divinity is "benevolent" in the same way that many other Western religions do. Pantheists and panentheists tend to see the sacred earth as a complex natural system that operates on the basis of physical laws. These laws structure the universe and create the conditions for life to exist, but they were not created specifically for the comfort and convenience of human beings. The same physical laws that shaped us and the plants and animals we eat also allow viruses that make us sick, shifts in the earth's crust that destroy our cities, and weather patterns that wilt our crops. Although there is suffering and death built into this system, pantheists and panentheists see the divine as experiencing our joys and our suffering along with us. A larger picture of harmony and beauty, of which human beings are only a small part, allows Pagans to reframe natural "evils" as necessary balancing forces that support the existence of life. Polytheists tend to share this latter perspective, as they see their gods as subject to complex natural systems in the same way that human beings are. The gods may know more and have more power than humans, but they are not all-powerful or all-knowing.

Pagans are more likely to see true "evil" as being the product of human actions. Although polytheists often understand the gods to be concerned with human suffering, they generally also believe that the gods respect the free will of humans and their right to learn from mistakes. The ability to act wrongly, as well as the experience of making amends, is part of developing self-responsibility and an internal moral compass. If the gods could play the role of parent through daily interference with devotees' free will, their worshippers would never cultivate their own virtues and become mature adults. Pantheist and panentheist Pagans also affirm human free will, and they often see "evil" as arising from unjust human systems. Systemic evil, such as wartime atrocities, genocide, human trafficking, and other horrors, are attributed to widespread distortions of values and disconnection from our essential relationality. The incorrect perception that individual humans are autonomous and independent, unaffected by the suffering of others or of the land, allows human beings to cultivate false virtues and even to advocate for suffering as "moral living." For many of us, it was only a few generations ago that severe corporal punishment (to the point of bruises and welts) was considered part of "good parenting"; today, such treatment is rightly considered abuse. Yet we are not free of our own distortions: many of us work sixty- or even eighty-hour weeks that degrade our health and take us away from our families, yet we justify our suffering as "providing for our children." Expressing love for family has become conflated with the pursuit, not of necessary material resources, but of luxuries. As Pagan leader Sam Webster remarks, evil is a result of the human freedom to make choices while remaining ignorant of the full consequences of our actions.[7] Without empathy with those around us, without a sense that we are part of a larger whole, human beings are easily deceived about what truly benefits those they love, let alone where their own best interests lie.

Starhawk writes about the problem of justice primarily in terms of power.[8] Our society, she states, is dominated by "power-over"—structures that place individuals and groups into rigid hierarchies where the dominant groups exploit and control those they oppress. She advocates instead for structures that encourage "power-with," ways of sharing resources and decision-making ability that benefit both the community as a whole and the individuals within it. She argues that scarcity— either the reality that resources are scarce, or more often, the perception that they are—tends to drive societies toward a power-over model, as those with power scramble to ensure their own survival at the expense of others. In a holistic, relational understanding of society, however, this behavior harms the selfish individuals as well by creating an increasingly unjust and predatory environment for all. Starhawk recommends the development of what she calls "power-from-within," self-knowledge and personal connection to the divine. Power-from-within sustains individuals in struggling for justice, and it is another way of describing the development of personal virtue and the discovery of the true will—a process of coming into harmony with the universe.

For Starhawk, the myth of matriarchal prehistory is a *soteriological* myth that illustrates power-with. Soteriology is the study of salvation—of how we might resolve the problem of unnecessary human suffering. The myth of matriarchal prehistory envisions a human society that is nonviolent, egalitarian, and living in sustainable harmony with the natural environment. Starhawk and many other Pagans feel that to recreate such a society in the modern day, we must embrace the values practiced by the Goddess-worshipping culture described in the myth. Other Pagans have been critical of this myth, for reasons discussed in Chapter Two. Yet it is not only feminist Pagans who are creating such myths of salvation. Others look to the opening of the Age of Aquarius for a global shakeup that will result in a new, more just society. Among Pagans, the belief that a definitive economic, environmental, health, or other crisis will force a decisive movement toward sustainable practices is fairly common. Many Pagans anticipate that the foolish choices made by humans on a mass scale will eventually backfire, ending the period of enormous first-world prosperity that Westerners have taken for granted, and forcing us to return to simpler living. Not all Pagans view this coming change in apocalyptic terms, however; some anticipate a more gradual pattern of change along the lines of the Great Depression, while still others optimistically predict technological advances, granting us clean energy and allowing us to slowly undo the environmental damage wrought by fossil fuel consumption. In all these narratives, however, Pagans see deities or the divine as working with human beings to seek justice. Justice cannot be imposed externally; it must come from within and among us.

Summary

Pagan ethics are based on the cultivation of virtues, rather than on following rules. Some Pagans think of cultivating personal virtues in terms of discovering one's true will, the unfolding purpose of a human life in conversation with the divine. A virtuous person is thought to demonstrate a state of spiritual flourishing that resonates throughout her life. Pagans are also actively engaged in recovering past civilizations' neglected virtues, such as honor and pride. In order for virtue ethics to produce a just society, however, communities need respected elders and ancestors to embody those virtues and assist their communities in creating ethical accountability. The lack of such elders is an obstacle for contemporary Paganism, where communities tend to be scattered and diffuse.

Some virtues, such as justice, must arise from community. For many Pagans, the essence of a just society is awareness of our interdependence with all of Being. Starhawk speaks of cultivating justice by focusing on power in relationships. She advocates working toward a society based on "power-with" and "power-from-within," rather than "power-over." Starhawk and other Pagans look to the myth of matriarchal history as a kind of salvation myth—in other words, a myth that contains a solution to human suffering. Other contemporary Pagans are mythologizing an anticipated global crisis that will trigger a shift toward sustainable living and more just societies.

Activities

On a piece of paper, list at least five people whom you admire. Next, consider the qualities that these people have in common. Write down these qualities as adjectives or adjective phrases, like "honest" or "good with people." Contemplate your finished list. How can you cultivate these virtues in your life? Does your community affirm these virtues? How can others to support you in your ethical development?

What virtues or ethical principles does your community affirm? What ethical controversies or problems it is dealing with? Consider how you might better connect your values or your community's values to ongoing disagreements. How can you balance virtues against each other when they superficially contradict? How can a community support both freedom and safety, or both compassion and honesty?

Create opportunities to gain occult knowledge of your interrelatedness. For example, visit a natural setting and sit quietly there, clearing your mind and focusing on your physical sensations and on your breath. Slowly shift your attention to become aware of the movement of life around you, and of yourself as a small part of a vast, living system. If it is helpful to you, you may wish to begin and end this practice with ritual or prayer. Be sure to allow ample time, as you may struggle with impatience or boredom before you can successfully open to your environment. (This practice is equally valid on an urban street corner, but new practitioners may find it easier to do in a less human-made setting. Classes and books on meditation may help in learning to quiet the mind's chatter.)

For Further Reading

Casey, John. *Pagan Virtue: An Essay in Ethics.* Oxford: Oxford University Press, 1991.

Coughlin, John J. *Ethics and the Craft: The History, Evolution, and Practice of Wiccan Ethics.* Cold Spring, NY: Waning Moon Publications, 2009.

Friedman, Ellen. *As Above, So Below: A System of Value-Based Ethics for Wiccan Clergy.* Seattle, WA: City University, 2011.

MacDowell, Katherine. *Ethics and Professional Practice for Neopagan Clergy.* Lulu, 2009.

Restall-Orr, Emma. *Living with Honour: A Pagan Ethics.* Hants, UK: O Books, 2007.

Conclusion

As I end this short book, I am painfully aware of how much more there is to say about all the topics I've covered, as well as the number of topics I did not address. I hope that this work is nevertheless an adequate introduction to doing Pagan theology, as well as to the terms and concepts readers will need to further theological conversation in their own lives.

Pagan theology is evolutionary in the older sense of the word—not to mean that it is growing ever more enlightened and complex (although I hope that is also the case!), but that it actively adapts to change. A Pagan theology that does not arise from experience or support an effective practice simply will not survive. It is in process, ever-changing as culture itself changes, adapting to the human condition in a complicated and fragile historical moment.

This book is also being written at an important moment in contemporary Paganism. The movement's rapid growth has led to an institutionalization crisis. Although many Pagans want infrastructure to support their religious practice, they are also afraid (and validly so) that the creation of institutions, formal theologies, and a trained class of clergy will cause their religion to stagnate. As I wrote for Patheos.com's collection *The Future of Religion,*

> Pagans frequently fear institutionalization because they do not want their religion to compromise its values (and their values are far from uniform). But the movement has grown too large; institutions will inevitably form in response to needs. In order for Pagan institutions to reflect non-mainstream values, they must be structured in non-mainstream ways. The struggle to creatively embed paradoxical values—individuality and community, professionalism and egalitarianism,

intimacy and inclusivity—into new institutions is
the primary Pagan challenge for the new century.[1]

It is my hope that creative institutional structures will
help Pagans nurture successful, vibrant communities. These
changes will alter Paganism as we know it today, but with a
combination of passion, practicality, and flexibility, a twenty-
first-century Paganism that retains its subversive spark while
better supporting the needs of practitioners is possible.

May this small contribution help to foster better
understanding of Paganism among both Pagan practitioners and
those of other religions. And to all my readers: seek the mystery!

Glossary

agnosticism: Belief that certain metaphysical questions, such as whether or not Deity or deities objectively exist, are unanswerable.

ancestor: A deceased person who is important to the practitioner. Ancestors of blood are those in the direct family line or adopted into the family line. Ancestors of spirit are those whom the practitioner admires or is inspired by, but who are not family members. Ancestors of place are those who used to live on the land where the practitioner now lives. Deceased people whom the practitioner knows personally may also be called "the beloved dead."

animism: Belief that all things (or sometimes, all natural or living things) have a spirit or soul, and that human beings share the world with other-than-human persons of many types.

archetype: In the work of psychologist C.G. Jung and mythology scholar Joseph Campbell, a pattern or symbol that is universal to human experience and that may offer access to divine reality.

Ásatrú: One of the better-known types of Heathen religion.

atheism: Belief in a lack or absence of deity. Somewhat interchangeable with "nontheism," except that in the United States, "atheism" is associated with hostility toward religion, while "nontheism" is often preferred by spiritual people who are not theists.

authenticity: Credible; legitimate; true to one's essence or spirit. The question of whether a historical grounding is necessary for authentic traditions is important to many Pagans.

BDSM: Bondage Discipline Sadomasochism (or, the D/S may also stand for Dominance/Submission). A set of consensual erotic practices performed in a negotiated relationship for the purposes of physical and sexual pleasure, or to achieve altered states of consciousness for spiritual purposes.

Burning Times, the: A historically-based narrative drawn from the work of folklorist Margaret Murray, arguing that those who were persecuted as witches during the medieval and Renaissance European witch hunts were practicing an ancient indigenous religion that had gone underground after the Roman Empire was Christianized. Some Wiccans believe that Wicca as publicized by Gerald Gardner is a modern survival of this indigenous religion. In scholarly circles, Murray's theories are seen as overstated or in some cases, fabricated.

ceremonial magick: A set of ritual practices derived from the Western mystery tradition (or Western esoteric tradition) that are concerned with refining the individual self, among other goals. Ceremonial magick draws on a long history of Western mysticism and includes elements of Christian, Jewish, and Hellenistic religion. See also *magick.*

cosmology: An account of the origin, history, and/or nature of the universe, often explaining the place of human beings in the whole.

Craft, the: A term for religious witchcraft, which includes both Wiccan and non-Wiccan traditions.

creation spirituality: A progressive Christian movement founded by Matthew Fox that focuses on earth-centered spirituality, mysticism, and artistic creativity. Not to be confused with creationism, the belief that God created the world six thousand years ago as told in the biblical book of Genesis.

cultural appropriation: The adoption of elements from a specific culture by an outside individual or group, particularly at the expense of the culture being borrowed from.

Dianic: Refers to feminist traditions of witchcraft and Goddess spirituality where only feminine images of deity are honored, never masculine ones. Dianic practices tend to focus on the sacred power of women's bodies, particularly with regard to the menstrual and reproductive cycles. Named for the goddess Diana, an independent figure associated with hunting, wild animals, and the moon.

Druidry (or Druidism): A group of Pagan traditions named for the Druids, the priestly elite of ancient Ireland, Britain, and parts of what is now France. In Druidry, groves of trees, bodies of water, and elevated landscapes are associated with various gods, goddesses, and spirits. Pagans who specialize in the revival of indigenous Celtic practices and beliefs often refer to themselves as Druids or (for those to whom historical accuracy is very important) Celtic reconstructionists. See also *reconstructionism.*

dualism: Belief that existence is made up of two complementary substances or forces. If these forces are understood as deities with whom one can have a personal relationship, the believer is also a *duotheist.*

duotheism: Belief in a complementary pair of deities, usually the Wiccan Goddess and God, of whom all other deities are aspects. See also *soft polytheism.*

eclectic: A Pagan whose practice is drawn from many sources, potentially including different Pagan traditions and other world religions.

ecotheology: Focuses on the relationship between religion and nature, often in the context of environmental concerns. Ecotheology is usually pantheist, panentheist, and/or animist.

elder: A senior member of a community who is empowered to teach, fill a leadership position (formally or informally), and/or serve as a role model. Elders are recognized by their communities, rather than assuming the title themselves.

epistemology: The study of knowledge, especially what can be known and how we know what we know.

eros/the erotic: A physical, sensual, and intimate expression of life force, identified in some Pagan and other religious traditions with divine love and creation.

eudaimonia: A term from Greek philosophy, sometimes translated as "happiness," but more accurately understood as "flourishing." The holistic well-being of a person.

gender constructivism: Belief that gender is wholly or largely based on socialization and can be very fluid.

gender essentialism: Belief that gender is wholly or largely based on biological factors and has little fluidity.

gnosis: Intuitions and information received from extraordinary sources. See also *UPG*.

Goddess spirituality movement: Also known as the spiritual feminist movement. Emerging from the political feminist movement of the 1960s and 1970s, Goddess spirituality emphasizes working with images of feminine divinity in order to empower and liberate women (and men). Not all spiritual feminists are Pagan; some are Christians, Jews, or members of other faiths. Among Pagans, feminist witches who work exclusively with feminine images of divinity often refer to their traditions as Dianic.

hard polytheism: Belief that there are many deities and that they are individual beings, separate and unique in the same way that human beings are. See also *soft polytheism*.

Heathenry: The reconstructed practice of ancient Northern European and Germanic religions. Heathens devote themselves to the Norse gods and view the Icelandic Eddas and sagas (originally oral poems recorded in the thirteenth century) as sacred texts. For some Heathens, the historical accuracy of their religion is very important; others believe that innovations are necessary to keep the religion relevant to the modern world. Heathens who are pro-innovation may consider themselves to be reconstruction-based rather than strictly reconstructionist. See also *reconstructionism.*

henotheism: Belief in and devotion to a single deity while acknowledging the existence of other deities.

idolatry: Veneration of images of deity, with varying attitudes toward how (and how much) of the deity manifests through the image. Often used as a derogatory term; "image veneration" is a neutral alternative.

immanence: A state in which divinity is manifest in the physical world, and all things are seen as an expression of divinity.

indigenous: Originating in or relating to a specific place. Indigenous religions both ancient and modern draw their practices and beliefs from the particularities of the land where their culture developed. Indigenous religions that are practiced in a location other than where they developed are called diasporic religions. Many contemporary Pagans are inspired by indigenous and diasporic religions and the way they model being connected to place.

initiation: A ritual designed to adopt a new member into a group, convey a spiritual experience, cause a spiritual transformation, and/or educate the initiate in religious practice, myth, or symbolism.

justice: A state of proper, ethical, and harmonious relationship within a community or society.

magician: A practitioner of magick, usually intellectually-oriented ceremonial magick (as opposed to practically-oriented folk magick, which is more often called "witchcraft").

magick: Ritual practices that are intended to alter consciousness and/or have a transformative effect on reality. The spelling "magick" was coined by early twentieth-century magician Aleister Crowley, who used it to differentiate ceremonial magick from stage magic. See also *ceremonial magick* and *religious witchcraft.*

matriarchal prehistory: A historically-based narrative drawn from the work of archaeologist Marija Gimbutas, arguing that Neolithic Europe was once occupied by a pacifistic, matriarchal, Goddess-worshipping society. In scholarly circles, Gimbutas's theories are seen as overstated.

metaphorical theology: In the work of Protestant theologian Sallie McFague, an approach where practitioners speak of God/dess using many different metaphors, such as mother, lover, child, or friend (not just the traditional metaphors of father and king). This approach is meant to help monotheists expand their sense of God/dess's nature.

monism: Belief that a single substance underlies all of existence. Compatible with both theist and nontheist belief systems.

monotheism: Belief in only one deity.

mystery: A truth or experience of the holy that cannot be put into words; sacred ineffability; divine reality that cannot be fully grasped by the human mind; a numinous encounter.

myth: A sacred story that expresses values, describes a worldview, and suggests modes of behavior.

nontheism: Belief in a lack or absence of deity. Somewhat interchangeable with "atheism," except that in the United States, "atheism" is associated with hostility toward religion, while "nontheism" is the preferred term for spiritual people who are not theists. Sometimes used for those who believe in a deity or deities but feel they have no relevance to humanity.

numinous: Describes the awe-inspiring and ineffable power and presence of divinity.

oathbound: Describes knowledge that an initiate has sworn an oath to share only with other initiates of a tradition.

occultism: Traditionally, knowledge of hidden or secret things, often requiring an initiation of some kind, and usually relating to the Western mystery (or esoteric) tradition. (See also *ceremonial magick.*) For feminist Pagan theologian Constance Wise, occult knowledge is creative, non-rational, subliminal knowledge that arises from the experience of the human body. Such knowledge requires special consciousness, usually achieved through ritual, to access.

oligotheism: Belief in and devotion to several deities while acknowledging the existence of many more deities.

oracle: A priest or priestess who acts as a medium for others to seek advice or prophecy from the gods.

panentheism: Belief that deity is present throughout the material world, but that deity is also more than the world ("God/dess is in all things, and all things are in God/dess").

pantheism: Belief that the world itself is a deity ("All is God/dess").

pluralism: Belief that there are many legitimate religious and spiritual paths. Or, belief that existence is made up of more than two essential substances or forces (this usage is rare).

polyamory: The practice of ethical, consensual nonmonogamy, both within committed relationships and more casual dating relationships.

polytheism: Belief in more than one deity. See also *duotheism, hard polytheism, soft polytheism.*

possession: A practice where a priest or priestess allows a deity to enter his or her body, often for the purposes of interacting with a devotional community.

post-Christian: Practitioners who remain engaged with Christian tradition and/or the Bible, but who feel that their beliefs and practices are too different from mainstream Christianity for them to consider themselves Christian. Some well-known writers in the Goddess spirituality movement are post-Christian.

power-over: In Starhawk's writing, power structured by rigid hierarchies where the dominant groups or individuals exploit and control those they oppress.

power-from-within: In Starhawk's writing, self-knowledge and personal connection to the divine that sustains individuals in struggling for justice.

power-with: In Starhawk's writing, power structured around shared resources and decision-making ability, aiming to benefit both the community as a whole and the individuals within it.

process theology (or process thought): Theology and philosophy based around the idea that the divine is constantly in a process of becoming and changing. In process theology, deity is fully present in the physical world, and all of being is participating in an ongoing divine creation. Important writers of process thought and theology include Alfred North Whitehead and Charles Hartshorne, both of whom influenced Goddess theologian Carol Christ.

queer: An umbrella term for a wide variety of sexual minorities and their allies, but primarily refers to gay, lesbian, bisexual, and transgender people (GLBT).

reconstructionism: Pagan traditions that use historical and archeological texts to reconstruct ancient religions, including Celtic, Canaanite, Greek, Egyptian, Roman, and other historical traditions. Some reconstructionists attempt to practice these religions in as historically accurate a way as possible, while others are more interested in adapting these traditions to a contemporary time and place. Pagans who draw on historical materials but are open to innovation may consider their religion to be reconstruction-based rather than strictly reconstructionist.

Rede, Wiccan: An ethical principle commonly phrased as "An it harm none, do what you will," where "an" means "if." See also *Will, the.*

reincarnation: The belief that after death, the soul (or at least one of the souls, in a multiple-soul model) is reborn into a new physical body, usually without a conscious memory of its previous lives.

religious witchcraft: The practice of magickal techniques (particularly folk magick, such as healing and divination) as an expression of Pagan religious faith. People of non-Pagan religions may also practice witchcraft or folk magick, but may not consider it to be part of their religion. See also *Craft, the* and *magick.*

ritual: In Paganism, a set of religious actions, usually heavily weighted with symbolism. Rituals may be wholly or partially spontaneous, or dictated by tradition.

Samhain: An originally Celtic holiday, now commonly celebrated as secular Halloween. The night of the year when the veil between the spirit and the material worlds is thought to be thinnest. Many Pagans honor their ancestors during this festival.

shamanism: A practice associated with indigenous religions where the practitioner seeks altered states of consciousness in order to contact spirits or gods on behalf of the community.

skyclad: Ritually nude.

soft polytheism: The belief that there is more than one god, but that the gods are in some way aspects of a single (or dual) Deity. Soft polytheist positions may include the following: 1) the gods are all aspects of one God/dess, who has both immanent and transcendent aspects (as in *panentheism*); 2) the goddesses are all aspects of one Goddess and the gods are all aspects of one God (also called *duotheism)*; 3) the gods are metaphors for natural forces that make up a larger Deity (as in *pantheism*); or 4) the gods are expressions of Jungian archetypes, through which human beings can experience an otherwise unknowable Deity.

solitary: A Pagan who does not regularly practice with other Pagans or belong to a Pagan group.

soteriology: The study of salvation and/or of solutions to unnecessary human suffering.

spiritual feminist movement: See *Goddess spirituality movement.*

syncretism: The combining of beliefs, practices, and symbols from different religions.

theism: Belief in a deity or deities, usually personal, i.e. a deity or deities with whom one can have a meaningful relationship, as with a person.

Thelema: A philosophy associated with twentieth-century magician Aleister Crowley. Thelema is not explicitly Pagan, but many Thelemites practice forms of contemporary Paganism. The Law of Thelema states, "Do what thou wilt shall be the whole of the Law. Love is the Law, Love under Will." The Wiccan Rede may be drawn from the Law of Thelema. See also *Rede, Wiccan* and *Will, the.*

theodicy: The study of evil, particularly regarding its origins and causes.

theology: An investigation of the nature of Deity, deities, and divinity; an intellectual framework for religious belief and practice; an organized expression of the meaning of numinous or sacred experiences. Contemporary Paganism has many theologies.

tradition: A body of rituals, liturgy, myth, and folklore on which Pagans base their practice. Within a single Pagan religion, such as Wicca, there are many traditions, such as Alexandrian Wicca, Georgian Wicca, Dianic Wicca, etc. Each tradition has its own body of knowledge, which may be recorded in a book and passed to new practitioners as part of an initiatory process.

transcendence: A state where divinity is seen as outside and beyond the physical world, utterly different from it.

transgender: Refers to a range of unconventional relationships to gender. Transgender people do not identify with the sex and gender roles they were assigned at birth, and they may feel that their psychological gender and physical bodies are mismatched. Some transgender people undergo hormonal treatments or gender reassignment surgery in order to take on the bodies and gender roles that they desire, while others consider themselves to be "third-gendered," neither wholly male nor female. The in-between state of being transgender is sometimes thought to be an advantage for shamanic work.

UPG: Unverified (or Unverifiable) Personal Gnosis, as opposed to Peer-Corroborated Gnosis (PCG). See also *gnosis.*

virtue ethics: An ethical system based on the cultivation of personal and community virtues in a harmonious balance.

Wicca: The largest contemporary Pagan religion. Wicca is a form of religious witchcraft. Most Wiccans are duotheistic, worshipping the Goddess (in her aspects of maiden, mother, and crone) and the Horned God. The religion was first publicized in the United Kingdom by Gerald Gardner in the 1950s, and it sparked the widespread revival of Paganism. Gardner's Wicca and its direct offshoots (now often called "British Traditional Wicca") have inspired dozens of loosely related Wiccan traditions, which continue to proliferate today. See also *Burning Times, the* and *Rede, Wiccan.*

Will, the (or true will): A unifying intention that expresses a state of alignment and personal contact with divinity; the unfolding purpose of a human life in conversation with the divine. Associated with Thelemic philosophy.

witch: A practitioner of witchcraft (usually Pagan). Many Wiccans and some other Pagans call themselves witches in solidarity with those who were executed during the European witch hunts of the medieval and Renaissance periods. Some believe these "witches" were practicing an ancient indigenous religion. Other Pagans believe this narrative is exaggerated, but they use "witch" as a descriptive term for their magickal practices. See also *Burning Times, the* and *religious witchcraft.*

witchcraft: See *religious witchcraft.*

Selected Bibliography

Abram, David. *Becoming Animal: An Earthly Cosmology.* New York: Pantheon, 2010.

-----. *The Spell of the Sensuous: Perception and Language in a More-Than-Human World.* New York: Pantheon, 1996.

Adler, Margot. *Drawing Down the Moon: Witches, Druids, Goddess-Worshippers, and Other Pagans in America.* Revised and Updated. New York: Penguin, 2006.

Anderson, Victor H. and Cora. *Etheric Anatomy.* Albany, CA: Acorn Guild Press, 2004.

Blain, Jenny. *Nine Worlds of Seid-Magic: Ecstasy and Neo-shamanism in North European Paganism.* London and New York: Routledge, 2001.

Butler, Edward P. *Essays on a Polytheistic Philosophy of Religion.* New York: Phaidra Editions, 2012.

Campbell, Joseph. *The Power of Myth.* New York: Anchor Books, 1988.

Casey, John. *Pagan Virtue: An Essay in Ethics.* Oxford: Oxford University Press, 1991.

Christ, Carol P. *She Who Changes: Re-imagining the Divine in the World.* New York: Palgrave, 2004.

Cleary, Collin. *Summoning the Gods.* San Francisco, CA: Counter-Currents Publishing, 2011.

Coughlin, John J. *Ethics and the Craft: The History, Evolution, and Practice of Wiccan Ethics.* Cold Spring, NY: Waning Moon Publications, 2009.

Crowley, Aleister. *Magick without Tears.* Tucson, AZ: New Falcon, 1991 [1954].

Dominguez, Ivo, Jr. *Spirit Speak: Knowing and Understanding Spirit Guides, Ancestors, Ghosts, Angels, and the Divine.* Franklin Hills, NJ: New Page Books, 2008.

Easton, Dossie and Janet W. Hardy. *Radical Ecstasy.* Oakland, CA: Greenery Press, 2004.

Eller, Cynthia. *The Myth of Matriarchal Prehistory: Why An Invented Past Won't Give Women a Future.* Boston: Beacon Press, 2000.

Farrar, Stewart and Janet. *The Witches' God: Lord of the Dance.* Custer, WA: Phoenix Publishing, 1989.

Farrar, Janet and Stewart. *The Witches' Goddess: The Feminine Principle of Divinity.* Custer, WA: Phoenix Publishing, 1987.

-----. *The Witches' Bible.* Custer, WA: Phoenix Publishing, 1981, 1984.

Friedman, Ellen. *As Above, So Below: A System of Value-Based Ethics for Wiccan Clergy.* Seattle, WA: City University, 2001.

Gaffin, Dennis. *Running with the Fairies: Towards a Transpersonal Anthropology of Religion.* Newcastle Upon Tyne, UK: Cambridge Scholars Publishing, 2012.

Gimbutas, Marija. *The Goddesses and Gods of Old Europe: Myths and Cult Images.* New and Updated Edition. Berkeley: University of California Press, 1982.

Greer, John Michael. *A World Full of Gods: An Inquiry into Polytheism.* Tucson, AZ: ADF Publishing, 2005.

Harrow, Judy. *Devoted to You: Honoring Deity in Wiccan Practice.* New York: Citadel Press, 2003.

Harvey, Graham. *Animism: Respecting the Living World.* New York: Columbia University Press, 2005.

-----. *Contemporary Paganism: Religions of the Earth from Druids and Witches to Heathens and Ecofeminists.* New York: NYU Press, 2011.

Harvey, Graham and Charlotte Hardman, eds. *Paganism Today.* London: Thorsons, 1996.

Hunter, Jennifer. *Rites of Pleasure: Sexuality in Wicca and NeoPaganism.* New York: Citadel Press, 2004.

James, William. *The Varieties of Religious Experience.* New York: Signet Classic, 1958 [1902].

Jung, C.G. *The Archetypes and the Collective Unconscious.* Second edition. Princeton, NJ: Princeton University Press, 1981 [1934-1954].

Kaldera, Raven. *Dealing with Deities: Practical Polytheistic Theology.* Hubbardston, MA: Asphodel Press, 2012.

-----. *Hermaphrodeities: The Transgender Spirituality Workbook.* Second Edition. Hubbardston, MA: Asphodel Press, 2009.

Krasskova, Galina. *Sigdrifa's Prayer: An Exploration & Exegesis.* Second Edition. Hubbardston, MA: Asphodel Press, 2007.

Lecouteux, Claude. *The Return of the Dead: Ghosts, Ancestors, and the Transparent Veil of the Pagan Mind.* Trans. Jon E. Graham. Rochester, VT: Inner Traditions, 2009.

Lupa, ed. *Talking about the Elephant: An Anthology of Neopagan Perspectives on Cultural Appropriation.* Stafford, UK: Immanion Press, 2008.

Lupus, P. Sufenas Virius. *All-Soul, All-Body, All-Love, All-Power: A TransMythology.* The Red Lotus Library, 2012.

-----. *A Serpent Path Primer.* The Red Lotus Library, 2012.

MacDowell, Katherine. *Ethics and Professional Practice for Neopagan Clergy.* Lulu, 2009.

McFague, Sallie. *Metaphorical Theology: Models of God in Religious Language.* Minneapolis, MN: Fortress Press, 1982.

Murray, Margaret. *The Witch-Cult in Western Europe.* Oxford: Clarendon Press, 1962 [1921].

Myers, Brendan. *The Other Side of Virtue.* Hants, UK: O Books, 2008.

Nicoll, Kiya. *The Traveller's Guide to the Duat.* Stafford, UK: Megalithica Books, 2012.

Paper, Jordan D. *The Deities Are Many: A Polytheistic Theology.* Albany, NY: State University of New York Press, 2005.

Patsouris, Laura. *Weaving Memory: A Guide to Honoring the Ancestors.* Hubbardston, MA: Asphodel Press, 2010.

Restall-Orr, Emma. *Living with Honour: A Pagan Ethics.* Hants, UK: O Books, 2007.

Starhawk. *The Spiral Dance.* 20th Anniversary Edition. San Francisco: Harper San Francisco, 1999 [1979].

Starhawk, M. Macha NightMare, and the Reclaiming Collective. *The Pagan Book of Living and Dying.* San Francisco: HarperSanFrancisco, 1997.

Stone, Merlin. *When God Was a Woman.* Orlando, FL: Harcourt Brace & Co, 1976.

Strmiska, Michael, ed. *Modern Paganism in World Cultures: Comparative Perspectives.* Santa Barbara, CA: ABC-CLIO, 2005.

Thompson, Sarah et al, eds. *Gender and Transgender in Modern Paganism.* Cupertino, CA: Circle of Cerridwen Press, 2012.

Turkle, Sherry. *Alone Together: Why We Expect More from Technology and Less from Each Other.* New York: Basic Books, 2011.

Whedon, Sarah. *Birth on the Labyrinth Path: Sacred Embodiment in the Childbearing Year.* Patheos Press, 2012.

Winter, Sarah Kate Istra. *Dwelling on the Threshold.* CreateSpace, 2012.

-----. *Kharis: Hellenic Polytheism Explored.* CreateSpace, 2008.

Wise, Constance. *Hidden Circles in the Web: Feminist Wicca, Occult Knowledge, and Process Thought.* Lanham, MD: Altamira Press, 2008.

York, Michael. *Pagan Theology: Paganism as a World Religion.* New York: New York University Press, 2003.

About the Author

Christine Hoff Kraemer received her Ph.D. in Religious and Theological Studies from Boston University. She is Managing Editor of the Patheos.com Pagan Channel, as well as an instructor at Cherry Hill Seminary, which provides distance education for Pagan leadership, ministry, and spiritual growth. Christine is an initiate of a religious witchcraft tradition and currently lives in the Boston, Massachusetts area. More of her work can be found at http://cherryhillseminary.academia.edu/ ChristineKraemer.

Christine would like to thank Patton Dodd for the invitation to develop this book; Sarah Twichell, Niki Whiting, Kathleen Mulhern, Henry Buchy, Holli Emore, and George Popham for editorial feedback and suggestions; and the students at Cherry Hill Seminary for providing ongoing intellectual stimulation.

Notes

Introduction

[1] A version of this list was previously published as the pamphlet "What Is Contemporary Paganism?" (2011), available at http://www.cherry hillseminary.org/wp-content/uploads/2012/01/WhatIsTrifold.pdf.

Chapter 1: Deity, Deities, and the Divine

[1] Reprinted as Carol P. Christ, "Why Women Need the Goddess," *Womanspirit Rising: A Feminist Reader on Religion*, ed. Carol P. Christ and Judith Plaskow (San Francisco: Harper & Row, 1979), 273-287. Available at http://www.goddessariadne.org/whywomenneedthegoddess.htm.

[2] Pierre Teilhard de Chardin, "A Note on Progress," *The Future of Mankind* (New York: Harper & Row, 1959). Available at http://www.religion-online.org/showchapter.asp?title=2287&C=2162.

[3] John 1:14.

[4] See Sallie McFague, *Metaphorical Theology: Models of God in Religious Language* (Minneapolis, MN: Fortress Press, 1982).

[5] See C.G. Jung, *The Archetypes and the Collective Unconscious,* 2nd edition (Princeton, NJ: Princeton University Press, 1981).

[6] Janet and Stewart Farrar, *The Witches' Goddess* (Custer, WA: Phoenix Publishing, 1987), 3.

[7] Janet and Stewart Farrar, *The Witches' Goddess* (Custer, WA: Phoenix Publishing, 1987), 4.

[8] Janet and Stewart Farrar, *The Witches' Goddess* (Custer, WA: Phoenix Publishing, 1987), 57.

[9] Aleister Crowley, "The Universe: The 0 = 2 Equation," *Magick without Tears* (Tucson, AZ: New Falcon, 1991), 52-63. Available at http://hermetic.com/crowley/magick-without-tears/mwt_05.html.

[10] Starhawk, *The Spiral Dance,* 20th Anniversary Edition (San Francisco: HarperSanFrancisco, 1999 [1979]), 41-42.

[11] Raven Kaldera, *Dealing with Deities: Practical Polytheistic Theology* (Hubbardston, MA: Asphodel Press, 2012), 43.

[12] Sarah Kate Istra Winter, *Dwelling on the Threshold* (CreateSpace, 2012), 21. Also available at *A Forest Door*, https://forestdoor.wordpress.com/2010/06/09/the-gods-are-real/.

[13] See P. Sufenas Virius Lupus, "Polytheology: Syncretism, Process Theology, and 'Polyamorotheism,'" *Patheos.com* 2 Aug 2010, available at http://www.patheos.com/Resources/Additional-Resources/Polytheology-

Syncretism-Process-Theology-and-Polyamorotheism; and "PantheaCon 2012: Super-Syncretism! Creating Connection & Preserving Diversity," *Aedicula Antinoi: A Small Shrine of Antinous* 31 Mar 2012, available at http://aediculaantinoi.wordpress.com/2012/03/31/pantheacon-2012-super-syncretism-creating-connection-preserving-diversity/. Expanded versions of these ideas are available in *A Serpent Path Primer* (The Red Lotus Library, 2012).

Chapter 2: Myth, Tradition, and Innovation

[1] Sarah M. Pike, Earthly Bodies, Magical Selves: Contemporary Pagans and the Search for Community (Berkeley: University of California Press, 2001), 169–70.

[2] See Chas Clifton, *Her Hidden Children: The Rise of Wicca and Paganism in America* (Lanham, MD: AltaMira Press, 2006).

[3] See Janet Munin, ed., *Queen of the Great Below: An Anthology in Honor of Erishkegal* (Biblioteca Alexandrina, 2010).

[4] Graham Harvey, "Heathenism: A North European Pagan Tradition," *Paganism Today,* ed. Graham Harvey and Charlotte Hardman (London: Thorsons, 1996) 51.

[5] See Kenneth Rees, "The Tangled Skein: the Role of Myth in Paganism," *Paganism Today,* ed. Graham Harvey and Charlotte Hardman (London: Thorsons, 1996), 16-31.

[6] John Michael Greer, "Myth, History, and Pagan Origins," *The Pomegranate* 9 (Summer 1999): 46.

[7] John Michael Greer, "Myth, History, and Pagan Origins," *The Pomegranate* 9 (Summer 1999): 47.

[8] See Christine Hoff Kraemer, "'Story' Is Only Part of 'History': Re-evaluating the Work of Marija Gimbutas," *Thorn Magazine* 1 (Dec 2008): 48-52. Available at http://cherryhillseminary.academia.edu/ChristineKraemer/Papers/1175643/Story_Is_Only_Part_of_History_Re-evaluating_the_Work_of_Marija_Gimbutas.

[9] John Michael Greer, "Myth, History, and Pagan Origins," *The Pomegranate* 9 (Summer 1999): 48.

[10] See Jenny Gibbons, "Recent Developments in the Study of the Great European Witch-Hunt," *The Pomegranate* 5 (1998):2-16. Available at http://www.kersplebedeb.com/mystuff/feminist/gibbons_witch.html.

[11] See Chris Klassen, "The Colonial Mythology of Feminist Witchcraft," *The Pomegranate* 6.1 (May 2004): 70-85.

[12] John Michael Greer, *A World Full of Gods* (Tucson, AZ: ADF Publishing, 2005), 5.

[13] Michael York, *Pagan Theology: Paganism as a World Religion* (New York: New York University Press, 2003), 13.

[14] Barbara J. King, "For How Long Have We Been Human?", *NPR.org* 11 Sept 2012. Available at http://www.npr.org/blogs/13.7/2012/09/11/160934187/for-how-long-have-we-been-human.

[15] Jason Pitzl-Waters, "Parsing the Pew Numbers," *The Wild Hunt* 26 February 2008. Available at http://wildhunt.org/blog/2008/02/parsing-pew-numbers.html.

[16] David Abram, *The Spell of the Sensuous* (New York: Vintage Books, 1997 [1996]), 25-26.

[17]"2009 Parliament Statement of Indigenous People," *Council for a Parliament of the World's Religions,* 9 Dec 2009. Available at http://www.parliamentofreligions.org/news/index.php/2010/07/new-release-pwr-statement-of-indigenous-peoples/.

[18] Michael F. Strmiska and Vilius Rudra Dundzila, "Lithuanian Paganism in Lithuania and America," *Modern Paganism in World Cultures,* ed. Michael F. Strmiska (Santa Barbara, CA: ABC-CLIO, 2005), 241-298.

[19] Andras Corban Arthen, "The 'Indians' of Old Europe," Lecture, First Church UCC of Somerville, Massachusetts, May 15, 2011.

[20] Starhawk, "Religion from Nature, Not Archaeology," *Starhawk's Tangled Web*, 5 Jan 2001. Available at http://www.starhawk.org/pagan/religion-from-nature.html.

[21] I am grateful to folklore scholar Sabina Magliocco for the insights she shared in her presentation, "Folklore, Culture, and Authenticity in Modern Pagan Religions," given for Cherry Hill Seminary as a pre-Pantheacon event in San Jose, CA on February 17, 2011.

Chapter 3: Knowledge and Devotion

[1] Constance Wise, *Hidden Circles in the Web: Feminist Wicca, Occult Knowledge, and Process Thought* (Lanham, MD: Altamira Press, 2008), 78.

[2] See David Abram, *The Spell of the Sensuous* (New York: Vintage, 1996) and *Becoming Animal: An Earthly Cosmology* (Vintage, 2010).

[3] For more information on initiation in contemporary Paganism, see Isaac Bonewits, "Varieties of Initiatory Experience," Version 2.2 (2005), *NeoPagan.net,* available at http://www.neopagan.net/Initiation.html; and T. Thorn Coyle, "Opening the Mystery," *Patheos.com* 23 Aug 2010, available at http://www.patheos.com/Resources/Additional-Resources/Opening-the-Mystery.

[4] John Michael Greer, *Inside a Magical Lodge: Group Ritual in the Western Tradition* (St. Paul, MN: Llewellyn Publications, 1998), 111-130.

⁵ Isaac Bonewits, "The Advanced Bonewits' Cult Danger Evaluation Frame," Version 2.7 (2008), *NeoPagan.net.* Available at http://www.neopagan.net/ABCDEF.html.

⁶ I have used my preferred terms here; alternatives to PCG include "Peer-Corroborated Personal Gnosis (PCPG)" and the simpler "Shared Gnosis (SG)." According to personal communications from practitioners active in the Heathen community, the term "UPG" has been in use in Heathen communities since at least the 1980s, but its first published appearance seems to have been in Kaatryn MacMorgan's book *Wicca 333: Advanced Topics in Wiccan Belief* (Lincoln, NE: iUniverse, 2003).

⁷ Jenny Blain, *Nine Worlds of Seid-Magic: Ecstasy and Neo-shamanism in North European Paganism* (London and New York: Routledge, 2001), 122.

⁸ See T. Thorn Coyle, *Kissing the Limitless* (San Francisco, CA: Red Wheel/Weiser Books, 2009), especially topics relating to soul alignment, cleansing, and complexes.

⁹ Luisah Teish, *Jambalaya: The Natural Woman's Book of Personal Charms and Practical Rituals* (New York: HarperCollins, 1985), 43-45.

¹⁰ Sarah Kate Istra Winter, "Discernment," *Dwelling on the Threshold* (CreateSpace, 2012), 85-87. An earlier version is available at http://forestdoor.wordpress.com/2011/12/09/discernment/.

¹¹ See Lee Junker, "Friends' Practice of Group Spiritual Discernment" (2005), available at http://www.quakerinfo.com/junker_discernment.pdf; and Patricia Loring, *Spiritual Discernment: The Context and Goal of Clearness Committees* (Pendle Hill Pamphlet, 1992).

¹² Helen Berger, "Are Solitaries the Future of Paganism?", 23 Aug 2010, *Patheos.com.* Available at http://www.patheos.com/Resources/Additional-Resources/Solitaries-The-Future-Of-Paganism.html.

¹³ Michael York, *Pagan Theology: Paganism as a World Religion* (New York: New York University Press, 2003), 72.

¹⁴ John Michael Greer, *A World Full of Gods* (Tucson, AZ: ADF Publishing, 2005), 118.

¹⁵ See Kenaz Filan and Raven Kaldera, *Drawing Down the Spirits* (Rochester, VT: Destiny Books, 2009), 266; Sarah Kate Istra Winter, "Fallow Times," *Dwelling on the Threshold* (CreateSpace, 2012), 36-37; and Satsekhem, "Fallow Isn't Just about Fields and Dreams," *Mystical Bewilderment* 16 Mar 2012, available at http://satsekhem.wordpress.com/2012/03/16/fallow-isnt-just-about-fields-and-dreams-pbp/. See also Sarah Kate Istra Winter, "Spiritual Specialists," *Dwelling on the Threshold* (CreateSpace, 2012), 11-12. An earlier version is available at http://forestdoor.wordpress.com/2010/06/07/spiritual-specialists/.

Chapter 4: Life, Death, and the Human Body

¹ Doreen Valiente, "The Charge of the Goddess," The Doreen Valiente Foundation. Available at http://doreenvaliente.org/2009/06/poem-the-charge-of-the-goddess/.

² Starhawk, *The Spiral Dance: A Rebirth of the Ancient Religion of the Great Goddess*, 20th Anniversary Edition, Revised and Updated (New York: Harper Collins Publishers, 1999), 20, 234, 267.

³ Audre Lorde, "Uses of the Erotic: The Erotic as Power," *Sister Outsider: Essays and Speeches by Audre Lorde* (Freedom: Crossing Press, 1984), 53-9. Available at http://www.womenstemple.com/EroticAsPower-article.html.

⁴ See Virginia Burrus and Catherine Keller, eds., *Toward a Theology of Eros: Transfiguring Passion at the Limits of Discipline* (Bronx, NY: Fordham UP, 2006).

⁵ See Dossie Easton and Janet W. Hardy, *Radical Ecstasy* (Oakland, CA: Greenery Press, 2004).

⁶ Many bloggers weighed in on this controversy. For a starting place, see Jason Pitzl-Waters, "Transgender Inclusion Issue Intensifies," *The Wild Hunt* 1 March 2011. Available at http://www.patheos.com/blogs/wildhunt/2011/03/transgender-inclusion-issue-intensifies.html.

⁷ Jason Pitzl-Waters, "PantheaCon Releases Policy on Limited Access Events," *The Wild Hunt* 10 Mar 2012. Available at http://www.patheos.com/blogs/wildhunt/2012/03/pantheacon-releases-policy-on-limited-access-events.html.

⁸ Cara Schulz, "Building bridges between Dianic and Trans communities at PSG," Pagan Newswire Collective—Minnesota Bureau 25 Jun 2012. Available at http://pncminnesota.com/2012/06/25/building-bridges-between-dianic-and-trans-communities-at-psg/.

⁹ For more on the evolution of attitudes around gender and sexuality in Paganism, see Christine Hoff Kraemer, "Gender and Sexuality in Contemporary Paganism," New Religions, *Religion Compass* Vol. 6 (forthcoming).

¹⁰ Claude Lecouteux, *The Return of the Dead: Ghosts, Ancestors, and the Transparent Veil of the Pagan Mind,* trans. Jon E. Graham (Rochester, VT: Inner Traditions, 2009), 162-180.

¹¹ William J. Murnane, "Taking It With You: The Problem of Death and Afterlife in Ancient Egypt," *Death and Afterlife: Perspectives of World Religions,* ed. Hiroshi Obayashi (Westport, CT: Praeger, 1992), 35-48; see also Jeremy Naydler, *Temple of the Cosmos: The Ancient Egyptian Experience of the Sacred* (Rochester, VT: Inner Traditions, 1996).

¹² Judith A. Berling, "Death and Afterlife in Chinese Religions," *Death and Afterlife: Perspectives of World Religions,* ed. Hiroshi Obayashi (Westport, CT: Praeger, 1992), 182.

[13] See Janet and Stewart Farrar, *The Witches' Bible* (Custer, WA: Phoenix Publishing, 1981, 1984), II.115-134.

[14] Laura Patsouris, *Weaving Memory: A Guide to Honoring the Ancestors* (Hubbardston, MA: Asphodel Press, 2010), 2-3.

Chapter 5: Ethics and Justice

[1] Janet and Stewart Farrar, *The Witches' Bible* (Custer, WA: Phoenix Publishing, 1981, 1984), II.135. The Farrars make a similar observation to my own about the "polarized pairs" of virtues found in the Charge (II.136).

[2] For resources on understanding the Law of Thelema, see "Do What Thou Wilt," available at http://www.dowhatthouwilt.com/main.asp.

[3] Brendan Myers, *The Other Side of Virtue* (Hants, UK: O Books, 2008), 44-50.

[4] Doreen Valiente, "The Charge of the Goddess," The Doreen Valiente Foundation. Available at http://doreenvaliente.org/2009/06/poem-the-charge-of-the-goddess/.

[5] "Ethics," *Encyclopedia Britannica Online.* Available at http://www.britannica.com/EBchecked/topic/34560/Aristotle/254721/Ethics#toc254722.

[6] Constance Wise, *Hidden Circles in the Web: Feminist Wicca, Occult Knowledge, and Process Thought* (Lanham, MD: Altamira Press, 2008), 94.

[7] Sam Webster, "Evil, Ethics and Freedom," *Arkadian Anvil: Hammering Out a Pagan Future,* WitchesandPagans.com 27 Sept 2012. Available at http://witchesandpagans.com/Pagan-Studies-Blogs/evil-ethics-and-freedom.html.

[8] See Starhawk, *Truth or Dare: Encounters with Power, Authority, and Mystery* (San Francisco, CA: HarperSanFrancisco, 1987).

Conclusion

[1] Christine Hoff Kraemer, "The Future of Contemporary Paganism: Holding Paradox," *The Future of Religion: Traditions in Transition* (Patheos Press, 2012).

CPSIA information can be obtained
at www.ICGtesting.com
Printed in the USA
LVHW081743010921
696689LV00020B/937